RETIREMENT
SAVING
MADE SIMPLE

D1415106

RETIREMENT SAVING MADE SIMPLE

THE 401(k)

Sage Advice to Create Wealth
in Your 20s, 30s, and 40s

Robert Kratzer Everett

Published by Advantage, Charleston, South Carolina.
Member of Advantage Media Group.

ADVANTAGE is a registered trademark and the Advantage colophon is a trademark of Advantage Media Group, Inc.

Printed in the United States of America.

ISBN: 978-1-59932-657-3
LCCN: 2016948660

Cover design by Matthew Morse.

This publication is designed to provide accurate and authoritative information in regard to the subject matter covered. It is sold with the understanding that the publisher is not engaged in rendering legal, accounting, or other professional services. If legal advice or other expert assistance is required, the services of a competent professional person should be sought.

 Advantage Media Group is proud to be a part of the Tree Neutral® program. Tree Neutral offsets the number of trees consumed in the production and printing of this book by taking proactive steps such as planting trees in direct proportion to the number of trees used to print books. To learn more about Tree Neutral, please visit **www.treeneutral.com.**

Advantage Media Group is a publisher of business, self-improvement, and professional development books. We help entrepreneurs, business leaders, and professionals share their Stories, Passion, and Knowledge to help others Learn & Grow. Do you have a manuscript or book idea that you would like us to consider for publishing? Please visit **advantagefamily.com** or call **1.866.775.1696.**

To my mother, the late Esther Kratzer Everett, for loving me,
encouraging me, guiding me, and sharing God's love with me.
To all my nieces, nephews, and cousins here and around the world.
May you use these principles to become more prosperous and happy.

TABLE OF CONTENTS

ACKNOWLEDGMENTS

Over the years, I have met, associated with, and worked with some amazing people. So many people have helped me that it would take me another book to thank them all. My prayer is that you all realize what an impact you have had on my life, directly and indirectly. From a work perspective, I have been fortunate to work at and with some great companies including Fidelity Investments, John Hancock, MFS, LPL Financial, Pension Design Services, and Northeast Planning Associates.

At Fidelity, I would like to thank those who encouraged me the most in my early years, including Robert Reynolds, Ruel Stanley, Ed Madden, Gary Burkhead, John Cook, Bruce Johnstone, Bob Stansky, Liat Rorer, Lyman Jackson, Ben Lewis, Janet Owens, Pat Hurley, Matt Petri, Barbara Paul, Liz Benotti, Bronwen Cunningham, Sandra MacArthur, John Costello, Dick Smith, Stephen Peterson, Kristin Polito, and the late Christal Holderied and Frank Parish.

At John Hancock, I would like to thank Jim Bowhers, Gary Cronin, Doug Baran, John Foley, Drew Tamoney, Barry Evans, Andrew Arnott, Tim Quinlisk, Tim Keefe, Jim Schmidt, Lisa Welch, Susan Curry, Scott Ward, David Eisenberg, Karen Zeff Rosen, Dave Rickards, Michele Giuditta, Donna Marsella, Dan McCormack, Ian Shields, Diane Hallett, Subhadra England, Mirsini Tzigizis,

Paula Cleary, Shannon Tobin, Jim Schantz, Libbie Gilbert, Brian Kondracki, Andrew Firmin, and Diane Patry.

At MFS, I would like to thank Dan Hartigan, Hal Bjornson, Dana McCullough, Aviva Yaffe, Jeb Collins, Collete Sagar, William Shaw, Kate Kennedy, Chris and Jeff Croke, Greg Scott, and Chris Doucet. I would also like to especially thank the group of retirement plan education specialists I worked with and who taught me so much: Cathy Penabad, Laura Adamsky, Crystal Barnwell, Brian Curran, Tom Curtin, Daryl Shaffer, Brian Bazley, and Joe Hager. Thank you.

At LPL Financial, Pension Design Services, and Northeast Planning Associates, I would like to thank Ed Hiers, Matt Eaton, Ben Hiers, Louise Brassard, Mike Hartman, Yvonne Green, Diane Coparanis, Christina Marchinke, Emily White, Gary Weeks, Felix Estrada, Andrew Firmin, Bryan Harms, Judy Gentile, and Debora Dussault. At Northeast Planning Associates, I would also like to especially thank all the internal associates and the advisors for their help as well as their stories, words of wisdom, and encouragement. These have been invaluable to me.

From a coach-mentoring perspective, I would like to thank the people who have influenced me directly and indirectly: Mark Waldman, Srinivasan Pillay, Anthony Robbins, Cindy Rold, Hal Elrod, Bob Proctor, Charlie Epstein, and Joe Robinson. I would also like to thank my Sandler trainers: Pete Oliver, Michael Flippin, John Rosso, and Bill Scher.

I would also like to thank my clients who I have had the great privilege to serve. Over the years I have been fortunate to serve some of the largest companies in the world. I have also been fortunate enough to serve and help people working two or three jobs to maintain a living. To every organization and individual I have served: thank you from the bottom of my heart.

From a personal-support perspective, I would like to thank my brothers, Emil and Jim, and my dear friend Lou Domenech. They have supported me with love, patience, and kindness.

From the publishing-of-this-book perspective, I would like to thank my brother Jim for the hours he put in reviewing my copy. I would also like to thank all the people at Advantage Media for making this book become a reality—especially Harper Tucker, Scott Neville, and Regina Roths. They have been a joy to work with.

While I have tried to thank and mention those I remember, these are just a few of the names I should thank. I apologize to the many more I'll think of later or have forgotten.

INTRODUCTION

The 401(k) plan may be the simplest and greatest tool of our time for people to grow their wealth for retirement. The ease of making your money work for you over time is one of the greatest advantages of the 401(k) plan. Participants who start relatively young can take a long-term view and begin planning realistically for retirement without feeling a significant financial pinch—now or in the future.

If you are someone in your twenties, thirties, or forties trying to reach an inspiring investment goal, then this book is for you. I hope you find it to be a friendly, nontechnical read that takes a dramatically different approach to 401(k) plans and your financial and retirement goals. My intent is to introduce you to the basic concepts and make it simple for you to understand 401(k) plans.

Why a Book on 401(k) Plans?

Today, with more than twenty-five years in the industry, I've dedicated my life to providing service to small and midsize companies and their retirement plans for their employees. I work with a large retirement plan consulting group through LPL Financial and within the regional firm, Northeast Planning Associates, in Cambridge, Massachusetts.

Over the years, I've conducted 401(k) meetings throughout the country, and I've spoken to thousands of people on the subject. These are meetings to inform, educate, and encourage employees of companies offering 401(k) plans to get enrolled.

But in spite of all my efforts and the attempts of the financial-services industry as a whole, we've still not done a good enough job of educating people—we've been too technical, we've used too much jargon. For years, we've tried to cram everything we could into a single one-hour employee meeting.

Previous books have tried to discuss all the technical investment terms and all the in-depth details of 401(k) plans. This has caused potential participants to be overwhelmed and confused. When you get right down to it, all that information is already contained in the documents you receive as a participant in a plan.

What's most important is to consider the potential for your money in a 401(k) plan between now and when you retire. Essentially, we're going to gear your brain toward saving and investing your money in today's marketplace—and throughout your life. That is why this book focuses on the very simple things you need to do to enroll in your 401(k) program and to deal with some of the psychological obstacles that have hindered so many people from saving enough throughout their lives. I hope to impress upon you the value of beginning participation as early as possible for the maximum benefit. I also want to help you decide how much money you should be investing and how you should be investing it. We'll discuss some of the psychology of investing: why people don't save in their 401(k) plan, some neuroscience in regard to saving and investing, and how you can visualize and use some of the neural tools (mental techniques to help us change our thoughts or thinking) that are available to you today.

While this book is not a general or overall investment guide, it does provide some basic guidelines to readers who need to make informed decisions. It's intended to be an educational tool to help people who aren't familiar with their retirement plan to understand

401(k)s. Even though this book is comprehensive, I encourage you to use other online tools or resources to get additional information because there is *always* more to learn.

How Do You Start?

Simply put, a 401(k) plan is a way to save for retirement by taking money out of your paycheck on a regular basis and putting it into a retirement account for you. This is probably the easiest way to save. Many people don't miss the money once they get used to it coming out—when it comes out on a regular basis (and before they have a chance to spend it).

Getting started is simple. The way to begin planning for retirement is by answering three questions:

1. Do I want to enroll in my company's 401(k) plan?

2. How much should I save?

3. How should I invest?

To get involved, there are three additional steps:

1. You need to get information on enrolling from your human resources or benefits department at your company.

2. You need to complete the form.

3. If the form is a paper document, you need to return it to your benefits administrator or human resources department. Or, if you're working online—which is now more typical—you simply need to click the "Enter" button on your computer.

That's it. It's not too complicated. No technical jargon so far.

Why Am I the Right Person to Tell This Story?

I've spent more than twenty-five years of my career in the investment industry, many of those conducting 401(k) plan meetings in one form or the other. And in those meetings, like others in my line of work, I was not passionate enough to get people really excited about this—some meetings had been boring enough to put people to sleep.

Picture me a few years back: A young, blond, good-looking guy (or at least that is what *I* saw in the mirror) just a few years out of school, wearing a white shirt, navy-blue suit, and a beautiful tie, working for one of the most prestigious investment companies in the country. I was an account executive, dealing with some of the firm's largest retirement plans, servicing them, and conducting employee meetings to talk about retirement.

In one of my first employee meetings, I showed up at the union hall in Ohio, where I was to talk with a bunch of steel workers that belonged to one of the oldest, best-known unions in the country. Essentially, my job was to tell all these men, most of whom were significantly older than me, to begin saving for retirement. Needless to say, I felt out of place. Thankfully, I was greeted by the grandson of one of the union's founders who suggested that I take off my jacket, roll up my sleeves, lose the tie, and "just talk to the guys." I was nervous, and without my coat and tie, I felt naked. Afterward, I was so thankful to the union leader because he had sensed my apprehension and made me feel welcomed. He had coached me, which enabled me to teach his members what they needed to do to become participants in their retirement plan.

Since that early presentation, I've spoken to thousands of workers across the country, in nearly every industry imaginable. You name it, I've been there. From coast to coast I've talked to prestigious law firms, drug store employees, airline personnel, electrical workers, trash-recycling mechanical engineers, midwestern truckers (at 5:00 a.m., I might add), DNA scientists, machinists, factory workers, people who bottled water for a living, university college professors and their staffs, private golf-course employees and groundskeepers, and casino employees—working all hours of the night and day.

After these meetings, I've sat down with thousands of employees to listen to their concerns and answer their questions. But with such limited time and so many people needing help, I know my efforts had not been as effective as they could have been or as I would have liked them to be.

That's why I'm writing this book—because it's critical to get this message out! If we're all going to have enough money saved for retirement, then *we must start now.* And again, getting started is as simple as obtaining the application form, filling it out, and turning it in.

Today, everything is easier because most of the time it's online—click, click, click and you're done. But in reality, you need some basic understanding regarding investments. That's another reason I want to share the wisdom in this book: so you can make better sense of all this.

Along with that, I feel it necessary to help people address their fears. That's why I'm spending a portion of this book addressing uncertainties, talking about how we view and respond to the ups and downs in the markets.

When I was conducting all those meetings at all those firms, I also came to realize that not everyone can save the amounts that they need to. So some of what I'll address in this book is that it's essential to understand that even a 1 or 2 percent deduction from your paycheck is a move in the right direction—especially if your company has a "match." (I'll explain what a match is later.)

So 401(k)s are not complicated; they are the real deal. The money that you save is your money—always.

In addition to the picture I've already painted about the 401(k) landscape, here are a few other reasons why I wanted to write this book:

1. Many of the existing books on retirement planning are for people a lot closer to retirement, in their fifties or even later. Those books begin by asking the reader to calculate how much they will need to live comfortably in retirement, and it seems absurd to me to ask a twenty-, thirty-, or forty-year-old what his or her expenses will be in retirement.

2. People generally don't understand how important it is to save. We have never been taught many of the simple investment principles that could make a significant difference in our lives. We have never been told how much we need to save in order to have a decent retirement.

3. While companies strive to grow or struggle to stay in business—and many companies don't even offer a retirement plan—those organizations that do sponsor retirement plans are chiefly concerned with their own products and services. Consequently, they may not focus on helping the participants in their plans as much as they might.

4. As individuals, we are focused on our families, jobs, and paying our bills *today*. Our brains want to live in the now. Everything we could ever want to bring us joy is only a click away—except our retirement. Thinking about retirement planning, saving, and investing typically has no place in

the now—especially if we're in our twenties, thirties, and sometimes even in our forties.

5. Most retirement planning books don't deal with how we respond *mentally* in regard to our investments, our outlooks, our future—basically how we make decisions and how those decisions may impact our future. Today, we're fortunate to know so much about the brain—what causes us to take action, what causes us to avoid taking action, and what we do when faced with fear. And this knowledge is paramount to dealing with the ups and downs of the market—the constant wave of plusses and minuses. It's time to look at this knowledge and how it can help us be successful regarding our retirement planning.

DISCLAIMER

The information communicated by, in, to, or through this book and your receipt or use of it: (1) is not provided in the course of and does not create or constitute an attorney-client, investor-advisor, or any other relationship, fiduciary or otherwise; (2) is not intended as a solicitation; (3) does not and is not intended to convey or constitute any legal or financial advice; and (4) is not a substitute for obtaining legal advice from a qualified attorney or financial advice from an investment professional. You should not act upon any such

information without first seeking qualified professional counsel on your specific matter.

This book's purpose is to cover principles and make general sugges-
tions about investing. All decisions that you make in regard to retirement, savings, and how you invest your money are ultimately yours.
I should also point out that, while I have many years of experience
in the investment industry, I'm definitely not a psychologist or a
neuroscientist.

For people already in a retirement plan, I encourage you to read
this book to make sure you're on track; I want you to understand
some of the basic principles and concepts that you need to review
and consider with your retirement plan. I'd also like to help you deal
with some of the psychological barriers that may be hindering you
from really reaching your retirement goals in regard to the amount
of money you need. And I want to help you see through some of
the clutter in the press and on the Internet and to see what really is
important.

It bears repeating: *the 401(k) plan may be the simplest and greatest
vehicle of our time for people to grow their wealth for retirement.* The
information in this book is geared toward people in their twenties,
thirties, and forties who work for a company that has a 401(k) plan.
It contains some basic information to help you make sense of your
plan and to help you see how basic, simple decisions can have an
unbelievable effect on your ability to have enough money in retirement. In short, it's my call to action to you: it's time for you to get
started on investing in your 401(k) now.

CHAPTER
ONE

WHAT IS A 401(k) PLAN?

A 401(k) is one of the simplest, easiest ways to put money aside for retirement.

So what is a 401(k) plan? It's typically a company-sponsored retirement plan, where money from an employee's paycheck is deposited into an account for the employee on a regular basis. The account is specifically for that employee's retirement. The funds contributed by the employee remain his or her money. The funds are typically invested where they can grow tax-free until withdrawal, usually when you retire.

Just having a 401(k) plan available to you as an employee is a phenomenal benefit. If you have one, you are lucky—many employees do not. As an added plus, some companies offer an employer-match program, which means they match the employee's contributions.

The concept of the 401(k) plan was established by the United States Revenue Act of 1978. As a matter of fact, it was established in Section 401(k), hence its name. However, it wasn't until 1981 that the Internal Revenue Service (IRS) issued regulations adding clarity to payroll deductions to allow employees to determine what proportion of their wages and salaries would be deferred to a retirement plan. By 1993, nearly half of all large US companies were offering 401(k) plans.

Today, more than seventy-three million workers are actively participating in a defined-contribution plan—of which a 401(k) plan is one—and assets in those plans total approximately $7 trillion.[1]

These 401(k) plans are important because the money we save is going to be essential for nearly all of us in retirement. It's critical to think about savings because according to *Moody's Analytics*, as reported in the *Wall Street Journal*, people under age thirty-five—generally known as the "millennial generation"—are currently experiencing a negative 2 percent savings rate.[2] Basically, that means they're spending more money than they're actually making. By comparison, people in higher age brackets are experiencing positive savings rates: ages thirty-five to forty-four save about 3 percent, ages forty-five to fifty-four save about 6 percent, and ages fifty-five and older save about 13 percent.[3] These are just *savings* rates, not *participation in 401(k)* rates, but we'll talk about the need to save more as we go through the book.

Interestingly, the Employee Benefit Research Institute in 2015 estimated that the median amount in a 401(k) savings account is about $18,433 and noted that 40 percent of participants have less

---

1   *Private Pension Plan Bulletin, Abstract of 2011 Form 5500 Annual Reports*, U.S. Department of Labor Employee Benefits Security Administration, Version 1.1 (September 2014), http://www.dol.gov/ebsa/pdf/2011pensionplanbulletin.pdf.

2   Josh Zumbrun, "Younger Generation Faces a Savings Deficit," *The Wall Street Journal*, November 9, 2014, http://www.wsj.com/articles/savings-turn-negative-for-younger-generation-1415572405.

3   Ibid.

than $10,000 saved in their retirement plan.[4] It's critical to understand these basic numbers because one of the major investment firms today, Legg Mason Global Asset Management, pointed out in a survey that US investors said they will need an average of $2.5 million in retirement to enjoy the quality of life they now have.[5]

While it's good for you to understand these numbers, for now, it's enough to ask yourself whether you want to participate and if so, how much you should invest and how you should invest your money.

Throughout this book, I'll make three major assumptions in regard to retirement savings:

1. **Social Security may no longer exist.** The first assumption is that Social Security may no longer exist in twenty, thirty, or forty years. This may be an incorrect assumption, but consider this: Social Security at its core is a system that was instituted in the United States in 1935, during the Great Depression, to help a small group of elderly people by providing a small supplemental amount to their other income. It's a program that's funded through a payroll tax, called the Federal Insurance Contributions Act (FICA) tax, or the Self-Employee Contribution Act (SECA) tax. And right now, we know that the system is running out of money—in part because what had been designed to provide a supplemental income to a very small set of people is now, unfortunately, providing the main source of income for many, if not most, retirees. This book is intended to help

---

4   Kelley Holland, "For millions, 401(k) plans have fallen short," *USA Today*, March 29, 2015, http://www.usatoday.com/story/money/personalfinance/2015/03/29/cnbc-401-k-plans/70383158/.

5   "U.S. Investors Need $2.5 Million for Retirement," Legg Mason Global Asset Management, March 9, 2015, http://www.multivu.com/players/English/7466451-legg-mason-global-investor-survey.

people be in a position to *not* need Social Security (even if it is still around).

2. **The retirement age may be higher than you think.** The second assumption is that people in the workforce today—people in their twenties, thirties, and forties—shouldn't really be planning to retire until age seventy, seventy-five, or eighty. This is due to two factors. The first is that medical technology today will allow people to live a lot longer. For instance, we are on the brink of being able to mass-produce and grow human organs using biotechnology, physics, and even 3-D printing. Breakthroughs like these in the field of health care may have us living to be 100 and beyond. So the assumptions in this book are that sixty-five (or the very small creep higher than sixty-five, which is considered by some to be a typical retirement age) is not a normal retirement age for people currently in their twenties, thirties, and forties.

The second factor to consider regarding a higher retirement age is that the age of sixty-five is an absurdity that was originally set in Germany—in 1916—and was designed for people who were disabled by backbreaking industrial labor, unhygienic (by today's standards) living conditions, and invalidity. America started using the age of sixty-five for retirement for Social Security in 1934—when very, very few people lived that long. Life expectancies then rarely went past sixty-five; today, we are surprised when someone dies so young. Yes, the government is now inching the retirement age higher, but I believe that rate of change is insignificant. It is still too young to assure that the system will be solvent in thirty years.

3. **Average salary of $40,000.** The third assumption is that the average salary in most examples in the book will be based on a figure of $40,000. Now while many people today make more than $40,000, I'm going to use this amount as a basis for many examples. So depending on your current salary, my hope is that you'll be able to do the math to make the examples applicable to you. For example, if you currently make $80,000 a year, then you'll just need to essentially double the figures in my examples. At the same time, readers making less than $40,000 will be able to divide their annual salary by $40,000 and then multiply the resulting number (which will be a fraction less than one) by the numbers in the examples.

So if you, for example, are making $38,000, you would divide that annual salary by $40,000 to get the result .95 ($38,000 is 95 percent of $40,000). Then multiply the numbers in the equations in this book by .95 to get your actual numbers.

401(k) Basics

Contributing to a 401(k) plan is, once again, virtually painless because your contributions are automatically deducted from your paycheck each pay period. Let's look at some other basic facts, features, and benefits of 401(k) plans.

- It's your choice when to start and how much to contribute. Even if you are strapped for cash right now, you can start with as little as 1 to 2 percent of your earnings. Participants can stop or start their contributions throughout the course of a year; you can do this as set out in your company's Summary Plan Description (SPD), which will be discussed later.

- Typically, the money is taken out of your paycheck on a pretax basis, which means it is taken out before taxes are deducted, so you save on taxes. But your company's 401(k) plan may have the option to contribute and save after tax. If you choose the after-tax option, you will not be taxed when you withdraw the money in retirement. In either option, the money remains tax-free while in the plan.

- There are limits for making contributions into a 401(k) plan in any given calendar year. For example, in 2016, employees could defer (contribute) up to $18,000, or 100 percent of their compensation, whichever is less. Participants age fifty and over could also make an additional (catch-up) contribution of $6,000 in 2016. These two amounts (deferrals and catch-up contributions) are typically adjusted annually for inflation and are usually greater than those you could contribute to an Individual Retirement Account (IRA).

- It's your choice how to invest. Usually within a 401(k) plan, there is an excellent range of investment options available for plan participants. Often, participants can choose from eight to as many as twenty-five (or sometimes even more) options.

- 401(k) fees may be lower than you might expect. They may also be lower than fees that a full-service investment firm would charge you as an individual.

- Employees retiring during the calendar year in which they turn the government's official retirement age or later may withdraw any or all of their funds at any time. Since the money is deemed for retirement, there is a penalty for withdrawing it early—10 percent on the amount you take out. You will also have to pay regular income tax on the amount you withdraw. Some plans do not allow early distribution except for hardship loans or withdrawals, nor are they required to offer this option.

- It's your money. The money that you contribute to a 401(k) plan is always yours. No matter where your career takes you or what happens to any company you may be with. You can take your money with you or roll it over into a new plan at your new employer. At all times, your 401(k) plan itself sits in its own trust, outside the company's assets. So, if something happens to the company financially, the money you have contributed to the plan is safe from any troubles the company might have.

Another important thing to remember is that often a company may match an employee's contributions (although this is not required). Sometimes this contribution is a set amount, such as fifty cents on the dollar up to 3 percent of one's contribution. In effect, the employer is giving the employee money. This is a great benefit, given it's free money, and it too will grow tax-free.

For example, for every dollar you're paid directly, you may see only seventy-five cents in a paycheck after the taxes are taken out. If instead you were to put that dollar into your retirement plan, the whole dollar goes in pretax (if you're saving on a pretax basis). If the company then matches fifty cents on that dollar, you now have $1.50

saved for retirement. Again, this is versus the seventy-five cents you'll have in your pocket if you had just taken that dollar in pay.

One thing that keeps younger people from participating in a 401(k) is that they're not planning to stay with a company very long. This is typical. They have great aspirations; they know that they're advancing quickly in their company, and they may want to move on to a faster-growing company. So they never participate. This is a grave mistake. Because, as I've already mentioned, you can take the money with you. The money is always yours.

Now, if your company does have a match, that portion of the money (the portion that the company puts in) may not be totally yours until you've been with the company for a certain period of time. This is known as "vesting." But, remember, if you leave the company, you can *always* take with you that portion of the money that you put in, plus or minus its respective gain or loss (plus whatever amounts the company has put in that has vested, plus or minus its respective gain or loss). Sometimes, you may be able to leave the money in the company's retirement plan, or at least you should be able to move it to an IRA rollover account at an investment company. An IRA rollover account is an IRA account that allows you to maintain your savings tax-deferred from your retirement plan.

In an upcoming chapter, we'll talk more in-depth about your options for investing the money in the 401(k) plan.

Getting at Your Money: Loans, Hardship, and Job Changes

Eighty-three percent of 401(k) plans permit hardship withdrawals, but only 4 percent of participants take advantage of this.[6]

---

6   "Benchmark Your 401k Plan – 2015," 401khelpcenter, http://www.401khelpcenter.com/benchmarking.html#.VlHgTb8Qjm5.

Your 401(k) is not a bank account. In some cases, having accumulated more than they have ever had before, some people get fixated on the money and, as my mother used to say, "It burns a hole in their pockets." Basically, these people feel they have to spend the money because for some reason they can no longer go without whatever their latest craving is. It is for this reason that many plans do not allow loans.

The 17 percent of plans that prohibit hardship withdrawals usually do so because the plan sponsor wants to have a vehicle that employees can count on for retirement. Not allowing loans or hardship withdrawals may also cut down on plan administration hassles and costs.

> Eighty-three percent of 401(k) plans permit hardship withdrawals, but only 4 percent of participants take advantage of this benefit.

While the idea of taking loans from your plan can sound attractive, doing so is *exceedingly* expensive! Loans delay and may even significantly keep you from saving enough or having enough for the plan's intended purpose: to have money for retirement.

Loans within a plan must have stated rules with which your plan sponsor must comply. Your plan sponsor may also be audited by the United States Department of Labor or IRS, the agencies charged with supervising 401(k)s for adherence to those regulations. The Department of Labor and IRS are very serious about making sure that the money is there for you.

While you may have put your money into the plan *before* taxes, when you repay the amount of your loan (made bigger by the accumulation of interest), you contribute back with *after-tax* dollars.

That means you earn the money, taxes are taken out, and only after you have paid taxes can the money then be used to pay down your loan. The interest you pay on your loan is also paid for out of your paycheck; you pay it to yourself. In short, with loans, there is no free lunch.

During the time your loan is outstanding, your money is also not working for you since it is not invested in the plan. It is not growing tax free, as it would be if it was in the plan. Consequently, your account balance will be lower, since the money is no longer in your account.

A loan might also be a time bomb for you with penalties and taxes. For example, let's say you take a loan for a five-year period, and then you lose your job, your company goes out of business, or you take another job with higher wages at another firm. In any of these instances, you may have to pay your loan back in full—within sixty days! If you cannot pay it back, the amount you borrowed will be declared to you as ordinary income, and you will be assessed an additional 10 percent penalty for taking the money out of your plan. So, if you put in pretax money, you will have to pay taxes on it. For instance, if you take out a loan for $10,000 to update your kitchen, and can't repay it, then you pay federal taxes on that money plus a 10 percent withdrawal penalty of $1,000 (for those younger than 59 1/2), which may only leave you with $6,300. You just lost about $4,000 to taxes and penalties. So be careful with loans from your 401(k) plan.

Once people start taking loans from their retirement plan, they also tend to be serial loan takers—meaning that they will go back again and again and take several loans from their retirement plan over their working life.

In addition to loans, the federal government also realized that people may need access to their money in severe hardship, so it allows people to access their money for extreme situations. However, your plan may still not allow you to access your money if it is considered too great an administrative or cost burden for your company.

For the plans that allow them, hardship withdrawals must meet a number of criteria: they must be for an immediate and heavy financial need, the withdrawal must be necessary to satisfy the need, you may not take more than is needed, you must first have obtained all distributions or nontaxable loans available under the plan, and you may not contribute again to the plan for a six-month period after having withdrawn money.

The following six reasons are considered by the IRS as acceptable for a hardship withdrawal:

1. Unreimbursed medical expenses for you, your spouse, or dependents;

2. Purchase of an employee's principal residence;

3. Payment of college tuition and related educational costs, such as room and board for the next twelve months for you, your spouse, dependents, or children who are no longer dependents;

4. Payments necessary to prevent eviction from your home or foreclosure on the mortgage of your principal residence;

5. Funeral expenses; or

6. Certain expenses for the repair of damage to your principal residence.

Hardship withdrawals are subject to income tax and, if you are not at least fifty-nine and a half years of age, the 10 percent withdrawal penalty. If you do qualify and do take a hardship withdrawal, you do not have to pay the withdrawal amount back, but you lose the advantage of that money growing tax-free until you retire.

If you leave a job before retirement, you have four primary options to consider with your 401(k) money. You could leave it in your previous employer's plan (if it permits), roll your money into your new employer's plan (if they allow it), move the assets into a rollover IRA or a Roth IRA, or cash out or withdraw the funds. Given there may be more options and there is a lot to consider, please investigate all your options by researching what to do with your old 401(k) money on the Internet. If you take your money and cash out, please understand you will be hit with penalties and taxes.

The Pretax/After-Tax Debate

Depending on the type of 401(k) plan available (some companies offer a choice), you may have the option of pretax or after-tax contributions. I'll discuss this more in-depth at the end of chapter 5, but for now, let me explain briefly.

Traditional 401(k) plans are pretax, meaning your contribution goes into your plan before you pay taxes on it. When you withdraw the money in retirement from a traditional 401(k), you pay taxes on the amount you withdraw at your tax rate at that time. So taxes are paid on the amount you originally contributed and on any earnings you've gained on those contributions on withdrawal.

Meanwhile, Roth 401(k) plans offer contributions on an after-tax basis, meaning you pay taxes on your contributions before you put them into the plan. Unlike the traditional plan, the money in a Roth 401(k) grows tax-free until retirement, so when you withdraw it at that time, you don't pay taxes on either the original contribution or any earnings on that amount (providing certain conditions are met).

Today, this is the great debate: should you contribute to your plan pretax or after-tax? There are many (very technical) arguments on each side and, as the purpose of this book is to make you feel comfortable with retirement fundamentals and not provide tax advice, the best we can say here is that there is no right answer for everyone. It's up to you as the participant. Either way you go, this decision should not be seen as a stumbling block to starting to save for retirement—now!

Choosing a Beneficiary

When you sign up for your retirement plan, your human resources or benefits person will most likely also give you a beneficiary form to complete to designate who gets your money in case of your death.

Many people never complete this form—or keep it up to date once they do complete it. We just don't wake up every day thinking about our death.

But the beneficiary form is just a document that makes it easier to pass your retirement plan money directly to someone or to some organization you choose. It allows the money to go directly to those you want, without going into your estate or through a probate court if you die without a will. It makes what can be a very difficult process into something very simple.

These forms usually allow you to designate more than one person or one organization. Usually, you just fill in the percentage of the money you want to give to each.

If you are married, your spouse is automatically the beneficiary of your money, but you still should add their name to the form. If you are married and want the money to go to someone else, you will need to have your spouse sign a waiver. If you are divorced and remarried, be sure to update this form with your human resources or benefits department—unless you want your previous spouse to get the money. Your spouse must also sign a waiver if you name your children as beneficiaries. However, most plans may not allow a direct transfer to a minor and the courts may have to appoint a trustee or guardian to get the money.

For those of you who dread even the mere thought of death, try to think of the beneficiary form as another signature the plan administrator needs, just another piece of paper. Even though this form is not absolutely necessary to enroll in your 401(k) plan, your human resources or benefits department may be after you to complete it because it could ultimately make their job easier, too.

401(k) Concerns

Before we get more into the nitty-gritty, let's address a few concerns people tend to have regarding 401(k) plans:

- **It's all just too complicated.** It's not. You just need to decide whether you want to participate, how much to contribute, and how you want to invest your money.

- **You lose a lot of money on fees.** The 401(k) plan can be the most efficient way to save. All plan fees must be deemed reasonable by plan sponsors, who must review all fees. And yes, fees must be paid to the vendors and service providers who deliver the plan to you—but they are often less than you might pay by going to a full-service investment firm. There's an entire chapter on fees later in the book.

- **You can do better investing the money on your own.** Some investors may do better investing their money outside the retirement plan. But it is also well known that the average investor does a lot *worse*[7]—because we sometimes think we can manage our money or time the market better than we actually can. Sticking with a long-term investment approach, such as the 401(k) plan, will provide greater opportunity for growth.

- **401(k)s are a benefit to only the top people in a company.** If a company matches employees' contributions, the company gets a tax deduction for the money it spends matching employee contributions. This is to encourage companies to sponsor 401(k) plans. That deduction is not unlimited, however; the company cannot use its matching contributions to unfairly benefit its most highly compensated employees. Simply put, if highly compensated employees' contributions into their 401(k) plans (and company matches) exceed a certain percent of *all* the employees' contributions (and company matches) into all of the company's 401(k)s, then the plan could lose its tax-qualified status. In which case, all contributions and earnings would have to be distributed to all plan participants. So, while a highly paid employee might contribute more to his or her plan, the company cannot favor them by providing matches that exceed amounts set by regulators.

- **Your money is tied up and you can't get to it.** This concern can be somewhat valid. But since the money is intended for retirement, think of it as being tied up for

---

7   DALBAR's 2015 Quantitative Analysis of Investor Behavior (QAIB) study examines real investor returns from equity, fixed income and money market mutual funds from January 1984 through December 2015. The study was originally conducted by DALBAR, Inc. in 1994 and was the first to investigate how mutual fund investors' behavior affects the returns they actually earn.

that worthy purpose. However, as we've pointed out, some companies do allow loans or hardship withdrawals for extraordinary circumstances. Throughout our lives, we'll encounter many periods where we may *think* we really need the money, but there's probably no time other than retirement when we actually *will* need it.

- **Too many rules and regulations.** Yes, there are a lot of rules and regulations. But that's why I wrote this book, to simplify them for you.

Sometimes, when it comes to thinking about our future, we are our own worst enemy. By delaying the decision to invest in a 401(k), we're just creating obstacles to a brighter future for ourselves. In the pages ahead, I hope to help you with some of the critical decisions you need to make in order to have a more confident retirement.

CHAPTER 1 TAKEAWAYS:

Check out these resources for more information on 401(k) plans. For answers to more technical questions concerning your company's specific plan, speak with your plan sponsor (typically someone in your human resources or benefits department) about the first two documents listed here:

- **Employee retirement enrollment book or resource.** These resources cover some of the plan features and what investments are available to participants. It also commonly contains the application form that allows a person to enroll in a 401(k) plan.

- **Summary Plan Description (SPD).** This document spells out in more detail all the restrictions, guidelines, and benefits of a company's retirement plan. With the SPD, you will also receive a Summary Annual Report. Once you have invested, you should also receive an annual statement of your account summarizing its performance over the preceding year.

- **401khelpcenter.com.** This online resource has a wealth of information for those who are considering, or are participants in, a 401(k) plan.

CHAPTER
TWO

THINKING ABOUT SAVING

In order to successfully reach any desired outcome in your life—in this case, your retirement saving goal—it is helpful to consider how you think about your goals, your fears, and how you might overcome those fears. In this chapter, we'll look at how delayed gratification, a positive mental attitude, and envisioning a better future are important components of overcoming fear and motivating you to take positive action.

Over the past year, I've reread a story about ten times about an experiment in the sixties and seventies involving children, marshmallows, and cookies. The amazing thing is, it was not just one article or book that I read ten times; it was in ten *different* books and articles! Clearly, it has a lot to tell us.

The experiment dealt with delayed gratification. In the experiment, researchers found that delayed gratification may be very hard for the vast majority of us, which makes this experiment extremely important to everyone who wants to be able to save for retirement because it goes to the heart of how many of us think about the future.

Walter Mischel, the renowned psychologist who led the study, conducted experiments to test childrens' willpower. He offered the test subjects various treats, one of the options being a marshmallow, to see if they could be left alone for fifteen minutes without eating the sweet. As part of the experiment, each child was told that he or she would be rewarded with a second treat if he or she did not eat the marshmallow when the researcher left the room. If the child could not resist the temptation, all he or she had to do was ring a bell to get the researcher to return, at which time the child would be allowed only one treat, not two.

Yet some kids didn't want to even participate once they were told the rules. They could not delay their gratification. They wanted or thought they needed to have their treat now.

In the marshmallow experiment, the kids held out on average less than three minutes! What it boils down to is that the kids in the experiment had trouble delaying gratification; they had little or no control over their willpower. Some of them squirmed, tried to keep themselves busy, or focused on other things. But the marshmallow won out in most cases. In fact, only about three in ten were able to delay their gratification—70 percent had trouble waiting even a short amount of time for what would ultimately be double the reward.

Where do you see yourself in this experiment? Would you have been able to hold out? Or would you have wanted to eat the marshmallow without waiting?

This marshmallow experiment reminds me all too well of an issue with 401(k) plan participants. Many participants seem to suffer from the same lack of control when it comes to money. Like the kids in the experiment, people who have the ability to participate in a

401(k) plan have instead decided to opt out because they cannot do without having their money *right now*. They feel they must always have ready access to it at all times.

I can't tell you the number of people over the years who have walked out of a 401(k) enrollment meeting stating that if they could not get to their money immediately, then they just didn't want to participate. This happens even when the company states it will match the participant's contributions. Foolish? Unrealistic? Yes! It's amazing the number of people who don't even want to talk about the subject of long-term savings, even when free money is part of the mix.

Is one in the hand really better than two in the bush? Maybe not. Think about it: in a 401(k) plan, we get quarterly statements telling us how much money we have. Just think what an adrenaline rush it might be to have money in an account you can see and that you might imagine yourself spending now. Think of all that you could buy or all the ways you could live your life. To me, that might feel exactly like a child indulging in marshmallows. Doesn't your mind perk up at the thought of that? Can't you just taste what life *potentially* might be like? What a mouthwatering thought!

Now let's get back to the kids in the marshmallow experiment. The researchers reopened their files some years later and found that the children who delayed their gratification seemed to be doing better in school. In fact, Mischel and his colleagues over the years published multiple papers on the topic and how the children who could delay gratification fared better in SAT scores by over two hundred points, had higher feelings of self-worth, and were better at managing stress.

So why is this important? Well, we must at all costs learn to delay our gratification if we are to build wealth over the years. We will need this money—and it is critical we learn some techniques to overcome the temptation to indulge ourselves and spend rather than save.

The reason so many people never achieve their financial goals—in fact, many rarely accomplish even short-term plans—is lack of commitment. They get distracted by whatever marshmallow is in front of them today, and long-term financial success never becomes a priority.

People also fail out of fear. These fears can be conscious, in that we are fully aware of them, or unconscious, in that they are due to programming or previous experiences in our lives that lie within our subconscious mind.

To achieve long-term goals and save enough for retirement, it's important to address both of these issues. You must learn to understand your conscious and unconscious fears and the desires that may distract you. This is not only critical for your ability to reach your retirement goals, but it's also important if you are going to reach all of your other life goals—financial and otherwise. Think about it: What's on your mind today that is keeping you from putting away money for retirement?

> It all begins with having the right attitude. Attitude is the first key to success.

So where do we start? It all begins with having the right attitude. Attitude is the first key to success. You must have a mind-set that you can achieve your goals, small or grand. Yes, there will be failures, and you may even have some tremendous or even horrendous learning experiences regarding what to do with your investments, but with the right attitude (and remember that even pitfalls can be learning experiences), you may achieve some great and remarkable things. The classic quote regarding attitude or having the right mind-set comes from William James of Harvard University, the father of modern psychology in

America who said, "…human beings can alter their lives by altering their attitude of mind."

Earl Nightingale, a founding sage of self-improvement awareness in America, may have put it best in his recording "The Magic Word," when he said: "And it works like this: great attitude, great results; good attitude, good results; fair or average attitude, fair or average results; poor attitude, poor results."

Nightingale also believed that success in life is our ability to follow a commonsense paradigm of rules. As he states: "There are guidelines that anyone can follow." And that is exactly what this book hopes to help you with—a set of rules to help you potentially reach your retirement goals.

Unfortunately, historically we have not been very good at helping young people develop their vision and think about retirement in a way that has the right attitude and is meaningful. In my opinion, it is somewhat funny to encourage twenty-, thirty-, or even forty-year-olds to trade any disposable income for savings *or* desire to earn more by showing them pictures of retired sixty-, seventy-, or eighty-year-olds in an aerobics class, swimming in a pool, or playing tennis. Think about it. We live in an age where people can quickly find anything they want by surfing the Internet—or they can easily hook up with someone very attractive by using an app on their phone. Those are marshmallows that can distract anyone from their long-term goals. I want to help you envision a better picture of retirement.

Envisioning Your Success

One way to reach your goals is to start with the end in mind. By envisioning the end goal, your desire becomes greater than the obstacles, divergences, and marshmallows you may face along the way. You should see your future filled with great possibilities. Imagine achieving your goals! In fact, try to actually become *obsessed* with them so that they are top of mind, in both your conscious and subconscious, as well as in your nervous system.

Having a great deal of money in retirement—or at least enough to live on—begins with seeing yourself being wealthy. It is about developing a picture of yourself doing things that you would consider to be fun and truly enjoyable in retirement. For some, that means being a millionaire or a multimillionaire. For me, it is living in a different country two or three months a year, with time and opportunities to meet new people, learn a new language, travel, and eat great food. It is also living a life without worry, enjoying all the people I am around, and learning new things. That is my dream. What's yours?

I've found that using some of the techniques set forth by renowned Harvard University psychiatrist and thought leader Srinivasan Pillay, MD, can be helpful. Dr. Pillay offers insights through his writings and teachings; he is a leading author and speaker who also teaches brain-based coaching for executives in the United States and other countries around the world. In 2013, Dr. Pillay's company, NeuroBusiness Group, was voted one of the "Top 20 Movers and Shakers" by *Training Industry* magazine.

One of the techniques Dr. Pillay talks about is *visualization*, or setting your sights on your ultimate goal and seeing yourself succeed in both first and third person as you move toward it.

Accomplished athletes often use visualization to win; they see themselves at the start, in competition, and then winning against an opponent. In using this technique to achieve your retirement goals, you must not only see yourself achieving your goal but also visualize your journey along the way, in first and third person.

Let's try visualization as it applies to getting started in a retirement plan. First, you must have the *desire* that you really want to have enough money. And you must make sure that desire is strong enough to take action. This may be as simple as seeing yourself getting the paper enrollment form or the web link you need to enroll online, and then walking through the basic questions we discussed in chapter 1. Ask yourself: Do I want to participate? How much do I want to save? How will I invest my money?

In this example, using first-person visualization, see yourself in your imagination through your own eyes obtaining that form or web link. In third-person visualization, take a step back from yourself and see yourself sitting down at a desk or a computer completing the application; basically, watch yourself doing the act as if you were someone else watching yourself.

If you are already enrolled in a retirement plan, visualize yourself taking the steps you need to increase your contribution amount. You can also use visualization to increase your savings annually by a certain percent, or you can visualize putting a reminder in your calendar to do just that. Whatever action you visualize taking, follow through by envisioning how the act impacts what you do and your future.

Once you have the image of yourself taking action in your mind, then you must actually perform the act itself. Try this exercise, then take action. Think it, visualize it, believe it, emotionalize it in your feelings. Obsess about it and take action. This is the key to thoughts becoming reality.

By visualizing your goal, your thoughts will connect to your actions, and before you know it, you will be enrolled and you'll be saving more for retirement. You can also use this technique to achieve other goals in life. Visualizing can also help those of you who are behind in your retirement planning and goals; just imagine yourself getting caught up.

Reducing Stress and Fear

Just as visualization can help you begin or advance your retirement goals, it can also help you reduce the stress and fear components of investing. Listening to the news and dealing with market corrections can cause a great deal of stress about money, especially if you have more money than you ever imagined you could accumulate. For some, these ill feelings are also ingrained by listening to others—friends, parents, or other family members—about their current or past experiences.

If you are stressed, worried, or filled with fear, then your thoughts may never become reality. Stress and fear can disturb coordinated brain activity and the way blood moves through the brain. The *amygdala*, which is the most primitive part of the brain—the portion of the brain that controls fear and anxiety—can send shock waves to the frontal lobe or the thinking portion of the brain. This can cause you to make bad decisions or no decision at all; in essence, it can cause you to shut down. When the amygdala takes over, a person tends to become aggressive, freeze, or run away from any given situation. People may find themselves making bad decisions because they are not thinking rationally.

Some people who are stressed about money never take action. In fact, they convince themselves it's not important to save or deal with their retirement plans or savings at all. Or they will make foolish decisions during periods of market lows or highs. Often these individuals will sell at market lows, when the stress is high, and then buy when the stress is gone, when the market is high. They may even become angry about their loss of money. These tendencies often are a clear indication that there is fear in one's subconscious mind.

So how can you use visualization to battle stress and fear?

You must first start with the end in mind and truly believe—beyond doubt—that you can reach your goals. Here again, you must be specific in regard to the amount of money you wish to have and the action steps that will get you there. It is not good enough to have a goal such as "I will be wealthy in retirement." *You must set a specific amount to have saved by a certain date.* Then create action steps to pursue that goal. Often, once your goals are more concrete, your internal global positioning system (GPS) will activate.

You can also use several techniques to reroute the flow of blood in the brain away from the amygdala—again, the fear or anxiety center—and get it moving to the frontal lobe, which as I said, is your thinking brain. These techniques will reduce stress and fear and significantly improve your ability to focus and make good decisions regarding the things you need to do.

I like to use Dr. Pillay's five-step paradigm, which he has named CIRCA. He claims these steps have actually been scientifically shown to change the blood flow in our brains, moving it from the amygdala, the portion of the brain that drives the fight-or-flight response, back to the reasoning center, where we can remain more rational. Here's how CIRCA breaks down:

Chunking. When you have a large problem, task, project, or goal, break it down into smaller pieces that are more manageable.

Ignore Mental Chatter. During two twenty-minute meditative or mindfulness periods each day, focus your brain's attention center (or "flashlight") on your breath, and ignore or just watch all the stories, thoughts, and chatter going on in your head without judgment. Just keep bringing your focus back to your breath, while sitting in a chair with your eyes closed.

Reality Check. When confronted with a problem, remind yourself that this too will pass. (This is the same advice my dad used to give me when I was growing up.)

Control Check. At those times when you feel totally out of control, remind yourself that there is always *something* you are in control of. I really like Dr. Pillay's analogy, where he says in essence, while we cannot control the ocean, we can surf the waves.

Attentional Shift. When you are stressed and feel lost, take your attentional flashlight in your brain and move its focus away from the thing that is stressing you to potential solutions to the problem or something else.

Research has shown that one of the best reliefs from worry is action. It's like the old joke, "Why does worry kill more people than work? Because more people worry." But, because you are reading this, it's pretty clear you are one of those who takes action!

So using Dr. Pillay's CIRCA technique to control the fear and stress that comes with wealth creation, try these exercises:

1. Start by breaking down the 401(k) enrollment process into smaller steps that you need to take so that investing for retirement is not overwhelming.

2. To gain more mental clarity in your life and become less anxious, take time daily to clear your mind.

3. Maintaining a constant reality check is a good technique to use when the market corrects or there is bad news on the TV. I know—easier said than done. But one way to reverse

a state of fear is by researching other market corrections. Then tell yourself, *Yes, this too will pass.*

4. Investing can sometimes be overwhelming. When it seems the markets or your investments are out of control, remind yourself of some of the simple things in life that you can maintain control over. The Serenity Prayer, Dr. Pillay points out, may help you when you are feeling overwhelmed: *God grant me the serenity to accept the things I cannot change, courage to change the things I can, and wisdom to know the difference.* Then, take control of your investments step by step, which I'll discuss in more detail in the chapters ahead.

5. Refocus away from the stressors in your life to the solutions. This is about being optimistic and looking for possibilities. When you are creating the life you want and desire, ask yourself how others have done it and how you can also be the exception to the norm.

You can learn more about Dr. Pillay's techniques for overcoming fear in his book, *Life Unlocked: 7 Revolutionary Lessons to Overcome Fear.* Companies can also look into his corporate training programs.

Studies of the brain have also taught us that fears and anxieties can be stimulated by other people because the mirror neurons in the mind almost automatically transmit consciously or unconsciously how other people feel. (Mirror neurons activate when you witness something occurring, and they make you feel as if you are experiencing what you're seeing.) This can be an important point to remember during market corrections, when there is a lot of anxiety around that may influence your thinking.

Remember—without changing your way of thinking, you may never change your life. That's why, to really have a significant impact regarding your future life in retirement, you need to understand how to visualize and pursue your financial goals as well as all your other goals in life.

Now, to really change your ways and keep on track, also remember that the brain needs to be given repeated instructions. So reading this chapter and this book multiple times may be the help you need to possibly reach your retirement goals.

A Better Future

Dr. Pillay also talks about visualizing a future life that is better than the present one, which can help change the direction of the actions you take today.

For example, young people just starting out in their careers who find themselves in jobs they don't like are accustomed to making their future condition much better. They take action by going back to school, working long hours, finding mentors, or getting additional certifications in their fields.

If you plant in your brain the idea that where you are with your retirement goals and your current saving for retirement is not good enough—that you want and believe you can have so much more in the future—then you will take the action steps needed to reach your goals. You can't just tell your brain everything is good now and then tell your brain that you want a better future, because your brain gets confused. You are sending two messages to your brain. This is why, in my opinion, so many people never achieve their retirement goals.

In addition, people who make excuses for themselves and tell themselves and others why they cannot save will most likely do nothing. Some are afraid to even try; they take comfort in telling others about their adversities, and they feel better not trying at all rather than trying and failing. The real winners in life feel good even when they fail, or at least they feel good that they tried. They ask themselves different questions: How do the *exceptions* do it? How do average people end up being millionaires or multimillionaires? How can *I* do it?

As your goals become clearer, the more likely you are to take the actions you need to take!

Having clear goals can also help when making daily spending decisions; they can help you avoid spending recklessly on an expensive car, buying $5 coffees daily, or having two hundred channels on your TV, versus potentially becoming a millionaire or multimillionaire. Those marshmallows that distract us are the things that we think will make us feel comfortable today. It is up to you to decide what you want and the way you want to live your life. What do you want to focus on?

Remember, don't be penny wise and pound foolish trying to save. Take the action you can take now. It is far more advantageous to focus on your better future and take action in that direction than it is to worry about things you cannot control. It is far better to focus on ways you can earn—and save—more money by helping your company grow by improving your skills, knowledge, and abilities.

CHAPTER 2 TAKEAWAYS:

Here are some exercises and resources to help you manage your mental chatter, whether it's helping you or distracting you from reaching your financial goals.

Visualization Questions:

1. Can you see yourself in retirement being a millionaire or multimillionaire? What will you be doing? Where will you be living and traveling? What kinds of exciting activities do you want to do?

2. Can you see yourself in the first and the third person taking the steps today that you need to take to be able to pursue your goal?

Suggested Exercises:

1. Take a minute to close your eyes, visualize, and see yourself in retirement. Create a lively, vibrant, emotional, exciting, loving, joyful, positive, and colorful picture.

2. Take another minute to see yourself—in the first and the third person—getting on your computer or smartphone to enroll, review your account, or increase your contributions.

Suggested Reading:

Life Unlocked: 7 Revolutionary Lessons to Overcome Fear, by Srinivasan S. Pillay, MD

Suggested Courses and Recordings:

If you are interested in learning how to manage your fear of failure, manage uncertainty, stop procrastinating, live a happier and more fulfilling life, and stay committed to your goals, you may want to consider purchasing Dr. Pillay's *The Untapped Power of You*, at nbgstore.com.

If you are interested in learning more about how we think and how our brain functions, you may want to consider taking the *NeuroWisdom 101* series of lessons by Mark Robert Waldman, which can be found at markrobertwaldman.com.

Companies that are interested in corporate classes may want to investigate NeuroBusiness Group, Dr. Pillay's training company.

You might also want to listen to "The Magic Word"—part of the *Lead the Field* audio series by Earl Nightingale.

THE MAGIC OF COMPOUND INTEREST AND INFLATION

In this chapter, we'll look at both the astounding magic of compound interest and the stealth killer of our buying power and wealth creation—inflation.

Compound Interest: The Magic to Wealth Creation

So what is compound interest? Albert Einstein called it "the greatest mathematical discovery of all time." This is where our money grows significantly over time—typically at a certain rate of return—and that growth compounds in magnificent ways. It is what makes money work for you. According to Investopedia:

> *Compound interest is interest calculated on the initial principal and also on the accumulated interest of previous periods of a deposit or loan. Compound interest can be thought of as "interest on interest" and **will make a deposit***

or loan grow at a faster rate than simple interest, which is interest calculated only on the principal amount.

The rate at which compound interest accrues depends on the frequency of compounding; the higher the number of compounding periods, the greater the compound interest.[8]

One of the greatest articles ever written on compound interest was authored by Richard Russell, a long-time investment newsletter writer. Written many years ago, the article, "Compound Interest, Making Money," may be one of the most popular pieces he published in his more than forty years of investment publishing. In the article, he points out several rules about making money, the first of which deals with compound interest:

One of the most important lessons for living in the modern world is that to survive you've got to have money. But to live (survive) happily, you must have love, health (mental and physical), freedom, intellectual stimulation—and money. When I taught my kids about money, the first thing I taught them was the use of the "money bible." What's the money bible? Simple, it's a volume of the compounding interest tables.

Compounding is the royal road to riches. Compounding is the safe road, the sure road, and fortunately, anybody can do it. To compound successfully you need the following: perseverance in order to keep you firmly on the savings path. You need intelligence in order to understand what you are doing and why. And you need a knowledge of the mathematics tables in order to comprehend the amazing rewards that will come to

---

8   Richard Russell, "Rich Man, Poor Man," *Dow Theory Letters*, August 5, 2014, http://dowtheoryletters.com/Content_Free/2494.aspx.

you if you faithfully follow the compounding road. And, of course, you need time, time to allow the power of compounding to work for you. Remember, compounding only works through time.[9]

As Russell mentions, he enjoyed reading what he refers to as the "money bible"—a book of compound interest tables. Today, we can actually use online calculators to play with this very simple principle. For instance, at Bankrate (www.bankrate.com), you'll find a very simple calculator that lets you enter your current wealth or savings and choose an investment return—maybe 7 percent—and see how that grows over time. (Under the **calculators** option, select **savings** and then **compound interest calculator**.) In fact, you can see how that money may grow by putting in the number of years you have between now and retirement to see how much you might be worth at that time.

Compound interest in itself is a very simple thing. It is an exact science. However, as you likely know, the market does not always operate so perfectly. I'll discuss markets later in this chapter and throughout this book.

For now, let's look a little more deeply at how much impact compound interest can have on our savings. Here is an illustration of saving $5,000 annually with three different scenarios. In each of these scenarios, I'm assuming a 7 percent return on your investment over time. This chart demonstrates how starting early is critical to one's ability to grow wealth over time. But really, it's never too late to start.

---

9   Ibid.

CONTRIBUTOR'S AGE	AMOUNT INVESTED PLUS COMPOUNDED INTEREST		
	$5,000 Contribution Age 25 to 29	$5,000 Contribution Age 40 to 75	$5,000 Contribution Age 25 to 75
25	$ 5,000		$ 5,000
26	$ 10,350		$ 10,350
27	$ 16,075		$ 16,075
28	$ 22,200		$ 22,200
29	$ 28,754		$ 28,754
30	$ 30,766		$ 35,766
31	$ 32,920		$ 43,270
32	$ 35,225		$ 51,299
33	$ 37,690		$ 59,890
34	$ 40,329		$ 69,082
35	$ 43,152		$ 78,918
36	$ 46,172		$ 89,442
37	$ 49,404		$ 100,703
38	$ 52,862		$ 112,752
39	$ 56,563		$ 125,645
40	$ 60,522	$ 5,000	$ 139,440
41	$ 64,759	$ 10,350	$ 154,201
42	$ 69,292	$ 16,075	$ 169,995
43	$ 74,142	$ 22,200	$ 186,895
44	$ 79,332	$ 28,754	$ 204,977
45	$ 84,886	$ 35,766	$ 224,326
46	$ 90,828	$ 43,270	$ 245,029
47	$ 97,186	$ 51,299	$ 267,181
48	$ 103,989	$ 59,890	$ 290,883
49	$ 111,268	$ 69,082	$ 316,245
50	$ 119,056	$ 78,918	$ 343,382
51	$ 127,390	$ 89,442	$ 372,419
52	$ 136,308	$ 100,703	$ 403,488
53	$ 145,849	$ 112,752	$ 436,733

CONTRIBUTOR'S AGE	AMOUNT INVESTED PLUS COMPOUNDED INTEREST		
	$5,000 Contribution Age 25 to 29	$5,000 Contribution Age 40 to 75	$5,000 Contribution Age 25 to 75
54	$ 156,059	$ 125,645	$ 472,304
55	$ 166,983	$ 139,440	$ 510,365
56	$ 178,672	$ 154,201	$ 551,091
57	$ 191,179	$ 169,995	$ 594,667
58	$ 204,561	$ 186,895	$ 641,294
59	$ 218,880	$ 204,977	$ 691,184
60	$ 234,202	$ 224,326	$ 744,567
61	$ 250,596	$ 245,029	$ 801,687
62	$ 268,138	$ 267,181	$ 862,805
63	$ 286,908	$ 290,883	$ 928,201
64	$ 306,991	$ 316,245	$ 998,176
65	$ 328,481	$ 343,382	$ 1,073,048
66	$ 351,474	$ 372,419	$ 1,153,161
67	$ 376,077	$ 403,488	$ 1,238,882
68	$ 402,403	$ 436,733	$ 1,330,604
69	$ 430,571	$ 472,304	$ 1,428,747
70	$ 460,711	$ 510,365	$ 1,533,759
71	$ 492,961	$ 551,091	$ 1,646,122
72	$ 527,468	$ 594,667	$ 1,766,350
73	$ 564,391	$ 641,294	$ 1,894,995
74	$ 603,898	$ 691,184	$ 2,032,645
75	$ 646,171	$ 744,567	$ 2,179,930

The second column looks at a twenty-five-year-old individual who saved $5,000 annually between ages twenty-five and thirty, to a total of $25,000. At age thirty, the individual stopped contributing to the savings account or 401(k) plan until, at age seventy-five, he or she was ready to take the money out. In this example, that $25,000 investment during those first five years grows to $646,171. That's how significant compound interest is.

The third column looks at a forty-year-old who begins saving $5,000 annually until he or she reaches seventy-five. In this example, that individual's $180,000 total contribution at 7 percent interest results in $744,567 for retirement. As you can see, this is only about $100,000 more than the individual in the first column, who started saving earlier and had contributed only $25,000.

The fourth column looks at a twenty-five-year-old who contributes $5,000 a year through age seventy-five. This person saving $5,000 annually is now worth almost $2.2 million. In total, to get to that $2.2 million amount, this person made a total contribution of $255,000.

Again, the power of compound interest cannot be overstated. It can have the most impactful, significant effects on your investments!

Inflation: The Stealth Killer of Buying Power

Inflation kills your buying power and savings. Inflation refers to a general increase in the price of goods and services over time; it occurs when the demand for goods and services (or the supply of money) grows faster than the supply of goods and services. This means more money chasing fewer goods and services, which causes prices to increase. Inflation is silent—it's like carbon monoxide as it kills off your buying power without you ever knowing it is there.

You probably remember your father or mother telling you how little things cost when they were young; maybe they told you how little a gallon of milk or loaf of bread cost when they were growing up. Or maybe they reminisce about how cheap their first car was (unbelievable, isn't it?) or how little a postage stamp cost. Of course, they also tend to align these stories with one about wages as well; seriously, could you live on what they made back then today?

Now, the price of everything does not go up year after year, but on average, over time, overall prices do rise. What inflation affects is our buying power over time. The buying power of the dollar overall decreases year after year after year. A dollar today will most likely buy very little when we retire.

As I write this, the cost of medical care and the price of a college education in recent years have skyrocketed.

Inflation erodes our buying power and should be a deep concern for our retirement planning. We need to be careful about what we earn on our money to stay ahead of inflation.

What causes inflation? It could be caused by the uptick in hiring in the marketplace, a rebound in the housing market, or by government-driven activities such as printing more money, buying more government debt back from the public, or just plain spending more money.

Whatever the cause, people worry about inflation when it is high and are quiet about it when it is low. Many investors don't worry about inflation when it's low since some of their investments tend to perform better during these times or because they just don't really notice how prices are increasing on a daily basis.

Inflation is typically low. Again, it is a *stealth killer* to our buying power and wealth creation. It is there constantly, decreasing our buying power year after year.

INFLATION CALCULATOR

If in **1990**

I purchased an item for **$1.00**

then in **2015**

that same item would cost: **$1.81**

Cumulative rate of inflation: **81%**

To illustrate how deadly inflation has been over time, in 2015 it would take $1.81 to buy what one could have purchased for $1.00 in 1990. So, $1.00 today will only purchase 55 percent of what $1.00 would have purchased twenty-five years ago.

Over the last one hundred years, inflation has averaged approximately 3 percent each year. Since this decreases one's buying power, let's take a moment to see what $40,000 would purchase with the impact of inflation over ten, twenty, thirty, forty, and forty-five years into the future. Again, I'm using $40,000 as a sample salary.

TODAY	$40,000
10 years	$29,764
20 years	$22,147
30 years	$16,479
40 years	$12,262
45 years	$10,578

This chart illustrates that, in ten years, today's $40,000 will only bring $30,000 of buying power. In thirty years, our buying power using today's dollar would only be able to buy $16,000 worth of goods and services. And in forty-five years, that twenty-five-year-old who's been saving all those years and then retires at age seventy-five will only be able to buy $10,600 worth of goods and services with his or her $40,000 salary.

So ask yourself, *How much will I need when I retire to maintain that $40,000 worth of buying power that I have today?* I'll address this question in greater detail in the chapters ahead. For now, the point that bears repeating is that **inflation is the stealth killer of our buying power and wealth**. In order to stay ahead of inflation, you may need to obtain an investment return greater than 3 percent, but even that may only maintain today's buying power.

A final note: today, if you're only earning 1 percent on your money-market savings at the bank, then you may be losing 2 percent of your money's buying power every single year. The rate of inflation going forward can do a lot of damage to your savings. Unfortunately, the inflation rate can't be predicted. Online inflation calculators let you try out various inflation-rate assumptions to see how much you really need to save. If you want to get an idea of how inflation might affect your buying power, check out Bankrate's online inflation calculator.

A Final Note to This Chapter: The Universal Law of Rhythm

Much like there are exact sciences in the universe—as we just discussed with straight line compound interest—there is also a law of rhythm that Bob Proctor, author, lecturer, business consultant, entrepreneur, and teacher, and who starred in the movie *The Secret*, talks about in regard to being a universal law: "This can be observed in the rising and setting of the sun and moon, ebb and flow of the tides, coming and going of the seasons, and in the rhythmic swing of consciousness and unconsciousness."[10] This law of rhythm is also critical to your investment success because the markets will move up and down throughout your life.

Markets fluctuate. They will alternatively contract and go on outrageous tears skyward. You must also expect great periods of malaise where nothing happens in the market and your investments go nowhere. Unfortunately, some of these periods have lasted for up to ten years. In fact, this happened in the mid-1960s, and it happened again recently. During the most recent period, they moved up and down, but overall they just moved sideways. Corrections in the market happen, and they will reduce the value of our investments significantly. But we should expect this, which is why Chapter 2 of this book (about the psychology of investing) is so important. You see, these periods just *are*.

To summarize, it is by investing over time with the aid of compound interest that one creates wealth. Yes, there will be cycles in the markets, but in the past these ebbs and flows have been small compared to the power of compounding, "*the greatest mathematical discovery of our time.*"

---

10   Bob Proctor, "Law of Rhythm," *The Science of Getting Rich Program,* PurposeBalanceLife.com, http://www.purposebalancelife.com/law-of-rhythm.html.

CHAPTER 3 TAKEAWAYS:

Here's an exercise for you to try using the Bankrate.com simple compound interest calculator. This calculator can be found at Bankrate.com and under the **calculators** option. Just select **savings** and then **compound interest calculator.** Feel free to try other equations as well using your own specific circumstances.

Simple Compound Interest Exercise:[11]

Pretend you are thirty years from retirement, and you decide to spend $10,000 more to get a nicer car.

Now, using the Bankrate calculator, how much would that same $10,000 earn you by the time you retire, assuming an average annual rate of 7 percent? If you decide to spend that $10,000 today on an extra bit of luxury, how much money does that preclude you from having in retirement?

If you understand compound interest fully, it can have a very significant impact on your life and your ability to create true wealth.

---

11   This is a hypothetical example and is not representative of any specific situation. Your results will vary. The hypothetical rates of return used do not reflect the deduction of fees and charges inherent to investing.

CHAPTER
FOUR

WHAT'S YOUR NUMBER?

Your *number* is the amount of money you need to have in savings for a confident retirement.

Now, nobody can say exactly what that amount should be, but it's probably more—maybe a lot more—than you think. Whatever your number is, your 401(k) can go a long way toward attaining it.

Again, nobody can give you an exact number; there are just too many factors to consider.

- Will your income grow consistently throughout your career?

- How much will your spouse contribute to your retirement savings?

- Will you be unemployed at any time during your career? For how long?

- When will you retire?

- What would you like to do in retirement, and what will that cost you?

- What will the rate of return be on your investments before and after you retire?

- What will the rate of inflation be?

- When will you die? When will your spouse die?

- What is the likelihood of illness, injury, or termination before retirement age?

- What medical costs may you incur in retirement?

- Will you need your money for any unknown disasters?

Clearly, many of these factors can't be known in advance; this is why no one will give you a hard, specific number. You can't predict accurately when you will die or if you'll be unemployed for a long period of time in the future. What's important is to realize that life doesn't always go as planned.

Now, if you are younger and read other retirement books—which, understandably, is not something most people devote a lot of free time to—many of them ask you to come up with a budget for your retirement expenses. Well, if retirement is twenty, thirty, forty, or fifty years in the future, that just seems crazy.

There is a better way. A better way to look at your number—the end-dollar amount you want saved for retirement—is to start with the end in mind. This number needs to be your brighter future, something that is realistic and that you believe is attainable.

Remember, you're young, optimistic, enjoy serving others, and enjoy working and contributing to society. You will most likely retire at age seventy or seventy-five, and you'll potentially live well over one hundred years.

So how much money will you want to take out of your retirement savings each year to help meet your expenses and still have enough left in the account to continue making annual withdrawals?

How Much Money Do I Need to Retire?

Well, my methodology is simple—so simple it will upset a lot of industry experts and maybe even scare you (assuming you haven't been frightened already). I'm sure you will find it eye-opening.

While industry experts cannot agree how much money you should plan to take out of your savings annually in retirement to live thirty years or so, for the sake of our examples here, let's look at a withdrawal rate of 3 to 4 percent. This may be an amount a person could withdraw steadily and also comfortably live on.

Four percent has long been the rule of thumb in regard to retirement-withdrawal rates; however, recent research seems to indicate that this might be a bit too much. That said, even if you do not expect to live thirty years in retirement because you know you do not have longevity in your genes, we will not take this number off the table.

Today, the better rule of thumb seems to be 3 percent. I believe it is more likely our money will last for the rest of our lives (approximately thirty years in retirement) if we withdraw our money at this rate. Remember, nothing is guaranteed. I personally believe it is likely that I will live past one hundred.

So now, without doing complicated math, if I only want to live on $30,000 a year in today's dollars, which means I have $30,000 of today's buying power, for my comfortable retirement, I will need:

$1 million

That's my number. What's yours?

One million dollars is my number if I were to retire today, in today's dollars, to give me a $30,000 annual income in retirement, if I withdrew 3 percent this year. This assumes no Social Security or government help.

It's a little scary, isn't it?

Let's look at another scenario: Let's say someone making $40,000 today wants to retire today. In order for that person to have at least that $40,000 annually to live on in retirement, withdrawing only 3 percent annually, he or she would need approximately:

$1.3 million

Think about this. I believe not many people are thinking about this very simple concept and what it might mean.

People operate under the assumption that they are all set. This is especially true if they don't think about it.

When we say we are all set, we have to watch how our own minds are playing with us, too. We are confident when we use that phrase, "all set," that we know our financial situation better than anyone else. We don't expose ourselves to the unknown, and we shy away from people who might take advantage of us under the guise of wanting to help us. Unfortunately, what we may also be doing is closing ourselves off from the truth as to what we may actually need to do to have a confident retirement.

We also may have psychological barriers to dealing with money and our future.

So let's take a moment and do some simple math. Put away your rationale and your excuses and see what your specific *number* might be.

Yes, I get it. You are not retiring today. You are retiring in twenty, thirty, forty, or fifty years. How much should you have saved by then?

That is the million- and multimillion-dollar question.

The truth is, given the stealth killer of our buying power—inflation—we will need a lot more money when we retire in the future than we now think we will.

The chart below shows you how much you might need. It is based on the price of goods and services increasing 3 percent a year over time. In this example, we will begin with how much $1 million will get you in retirement income today.

YEARS TO RETIREMENT	$1 MILLION ADJUSTED FOR INFLATION	3 PERCENT WITHDRAWAL	BUYING POWER BASED ON TODAY'S DOLLAR
Today	$1,000,000	$30,000	$30,000
10	$1,343,916	$40,317	$30,000
20	$1,806,111	$54,183	$30,000
30	$2,427,262	$72,818	$30,000
40	$3,262,038	$97,861	$30,000
50	$4,383,906	$131,517	$30,000

The "$1 million adjusted for inflation" column shows how much you will need, depending on the number of years from now until you retire. The "3 percent withdrawal" column shows how much you will need to withdraw years from now (the "Years to retirement" column) to have the equivalent of $30,000 of buying power, based on today's dollar. If you want, need, or desire $30,000 of buying power in retirement, how much money will you need to have for retirement?

By examining the chart, we can see that a twenty-year-old who is going to retire in fifty years at age seventy will need to be able to withdraw $131,517 annually to buy an equivalent amount of goods and services ($30,000) based on today's dollar. He or she may also likely need to have saved and accumulated $4.4 million in retirement savings to maintain that buying power throughout retirement. Of course, if this individual wants $60,000 of today's buying power in retirement, he or she may need to double these numbers.

Now, there is good news. Typically, as we work, our salaries have an inflation adjuster each year; many companies increase salaries yearly based on inflation or merit increases. As we get more experience and add more value to the workforce, we should also earn more.

We also need to save and invest wisely if we are to hit these goals, and we will talk about that later in this book. Remember, too, from the previous chapter, we need to let the compounding effect work for us, as it will have a tremendous impact on our savings. That is one of the secrets and magic to investing.

So looking at the chart, do you have your number? If not, find it and circle it or write it in the margin of this book or in the note section in your e-reader. This is important to move forward.

Next, we will study the effect of saving over time, compound interest, and how much we will need to save to obtain this amount.

And, yes, I believe it *is* achievable.

CHAPTER 4 TAKEAWAYS:

After reading this chapter, take these steps to figure out what your retirement savings goal number might be:

1. Go back and look at the table in this chapter.

2. Estimate the number of years until you retire. For example, let's say you will retire in thirty years.

3. Look at the column "$1 million adjusted for inflation" to determine how much you will need to save in order to have $30,000 worth of buying power in today's dollars. If you're retiring in thirty years, you will most likely need $2.4 million.

4. Then estimate what you might need in savings if you wanted $60,000 worth of buying power in retirement. In the example we're using here—yes, double it—you will need $4.8 million.

CHAPTER
FIVE

HOW MUCH SHOULD YOU SAVE?

How much should you save is the million- or, rather, multimillion-dollar question.

How much you should save is a lot more than most people are now telling you. Here, we can only estimate. There is no simple, singular right answer.

If you are starting out and saving money is a real burden, you may find putting away even 1 percent may seem to be a challenge. But even this small amount can make a big difference.

The average contribution made by employers to their 401(k) plans is 2.7 percent of an employee's pay. While some employers match dollar for dollar up to a specific percentage of an employee's pay, the most common type of match is fifty cents on the dollar. Nearly half (43 percent) of employees say that the match is the

The average contribution made by employers to their 401(k) plans is 2.7 percent of an employee's pay. While some employers match dollar for dollar up to a specific percentage of an employee's pay, the most common type of match is fifty cents on the dollar. Nearly half (43 percent) of employees say that the match is the primary reason for their participation in a plan.

primary reason for their participation in a plan.[12]

Years ago, I met with a single mother who became one of my 401(k) heroes. At the time, she was living with her mother and working two minimum-wage jobs—one in a casino and one in a shopping mall across the street from the casino. The single mother understood she needed to do *something*, so 1 percent was her starting point. Despite everything going on in her life, she was giving it her all and still understood she needed to plan for the future. She had more than her share of reasons why she shouldn't participate in her company's retirement plan, but she took the plunge and enrolled anyway. She was lucky. Her company matched that 1 percent dollar for dollar.

I cannot tell you how many times I've heard from employees that someone told them they should only save up to the amount of their company's matching contribution.

---

12   "Benchmark Your 401k Plan – 2015," 401khelpcenter, http://www.401khelpcenter.com/benchmarking.html#.VIHgTb8Qjm5.

While this is good-intentioned advice, it is, to me, a formula for disaster. Because it simply will not be enough.

Sure, if you are just signing up and contributing whatever amount your company might match, that is definitely something you should aim for at first, even if you feel it's too much. I mean, it's foolish to leave money on the table if your company is willing to give it to you. Remember, your money is your money, and you can increase your contribution whenever your budget allows or your plan stipulates.

So how much should you save?

Well, the *minimum,* according to some industry experts, is 10 percent. However, the new norm, given that most people may not have Social Security when they retire, is becoming 15 percent!

As Robert L. Reynolds, president and CEO at Putnam Investments and Great-West Financial, stated in a LinkedIn article, "I strongly believe that over time, taking into account the uncertain future of Social Security, saving 15 percent of income may need to become the new norm."[13]

In fact, our savings rate overall for retirement is so low that another industry expert—Bill Bernstein—believes that the savings rate should be mandatory: "So, you mandate that they [employees] have to save 10 percent or 15 percent out of their salary and put it into their retirement portfolio."[14]

I would actually go further and encourage those of you who can to save *20 percent.* The lower savings rate assumes you will always be working and in great health. And for some, that will not be the case.

---

13   Robert L. Reynolds, "Great ideas like the 401(k) must evolve to meet new challenges," *LinkedIn,* April 7, 2015, accessed September 27, 2015, https://www.linkedin.com/pulse/great-ideas-must-evolve-robert-l-reynolds.

14   Christine Benz, "Bernstein: Solutions to the Retirement Crisis," *Morningstar,* October 23, 2014, http://www.morningstar.com/cover/videocenter.aspx?id=670507.

For anyone just to *start out* by saving 10, 15, or 20 percent, however, may be too much of a financial burden. That's why I encourage people to save what they can and increase their savings by 1 percent of their salary every year. Before you know it, you will be well on your way to saving a good sum for your retirement.

So, for now, save what you can. Feel great about it, and plan to save more as you can. Remember, winners feel great about taking the little steps along the way.

The good news is that a lot of companies in the industry are trying to provide participants in a 401(k) plan with guidance on how much each person specifically should be saving. However, in my opinion, the formulas they often use are riddled with assumptions. In fact, they have to be; they need to make assumptions about the rate of inflation, the rate your money will grow, how much you may get in an annual salary increase, what amount you may consistently save, and how much you may increase that figure each year. The companies calculating these estimates also understand this and may tell you (most likely in a footnote that you are unlikely to read) what their assumptions are and what your probability of success will be with those assumptions.

Remember, though, that no one can predict the future—and the only "probability of success" that really matters is the likelihood that your money will be there for you when you need it! That's why our attitude about what we can do and achieve is so important.

Just the other day, I picked up a chart book with all sorts of retirement scenarios. The company had included its assumptions in it. One example featured a chart illustrating withdrawal rates of a retirement account. It stated that, if such-and-such happened and this-and-that happened, participants could expect an 80 percent probability that they would have saved enough money to live on for the rest of their life.

Does 80 percent sound good? I'm not sure. I have heard Charlie Epstein, another industry expert who wrote the book *Paychecks for Life: How to Turn Your 401(k) into a Paycheck Manufacturing Company*, ask people if they would ever get on a plane from New York to Los Angeles if they knew they only had an 80 percent chance of making it. Yet this is how we approach our retirement.

Therefore, while I cannot predict better results, **you must do everything you can to SAVE. Now!**

So once again, start by saving what you can. Later in the book, we will look at whether you are on track and if your savings rate is enough for you to have a confident retirement.

However, we all know life does not work with straight-line assumptions. It works like the ebb and flow of the tides, the seasons, and, at times, our physical, mental, and emotional states. That is why my savings target for some people is 20 percent.

I realize that there are some professionals making a great deal of money who might not be able to put 15 or 20 percent into their retirement plans. Why? Because the amount you can save in your retirement plan is capped each year by the government. If you are one of these individuals, I encourage you to seek professional financial advice to see how you can save and invest your additional money for retirement. The upper limit you can contribute to your retirement plan can be found on the Internet and should also be available through your benefits or human resources departments within your company. And people over fifty years of age may also make an additional contribution.

Roth 401(k) vs. Regular/Traditional 401(k)

As I mentioned earlier in the book, some companies offer their employees the choice to save for retirement with pretax dollars, which is referred to as a regular/traditional 401(k), or after-tax dollars, which is referred to as a Roth 401(k).

Most companies offer a regular/traditional 401(k), which means your savings are taken out of your paycheck today, before your taxes are calculated. So you don't pay taxes on the amount you save when you contribute that money to your retirement plan, nor do you pay taxes on all the potential growth on your retirement plan savings over the years. But you *do* pay the taxes on that money when you withdraw it in retirement—based on the amount of your withdrawal.

A lot of people close to retirement see this as a good option; they are hoping their taxes will be lower in retirement, since they expect they will have less income and be in a lower tax bracket.

The Roth 401(k) option allows people to pay taxes on their income today before contributing it to their retirement plan, thereby avoiding being taxed when the money is withdrawn in retirement—*as the laws stand now.* Many younger people prefer this plan because they want to pay taxes as they're earning the money, before it goes into the company's plan, rather than later during retirement.

For example, by using the Roth 401(k) option, a single person making $40,000 a year in the 25 percent tax bracket and saving 15 percent of his or her income in a company's retirement plan would most likely pay an additional $1,500 in taxes per year until retirement in order to have tax-free money at that time.

Which one is right for you? It's hard to say. We don't know what the tax rates will be that many years from now, so it's hard to gauge whether the Roth 401(k) is a better deal or not. Taxes are determined by Congress and at some point—really any point—legisla-tors can change how even your Roth money may be taxed over the next twenty, thirty, or forty years. Just look at Social Security, which was not originally meant to be taxed, but which now, depending on your situation—usually income from other sources—may indeed be partially taxable. So Congress has the power to tax, and as we all know, no one knows for certain what it may do in the future.

CHAPTER 5 TAKEAWAYS:

Take Action:

If you are just getting started: Start small, pick a reasonable amount, and feel great about getting started. Remember, most people cannot just start saving 15 percent immediately. We just don't budget or change our buying and savings habits that quickly. Many people starting off will do all they can to maximize what their company may match on their contributions, provided their company has a match.

If you are already participating in your company's retirement plan: See what your number is, and consider increasing that amount now if you can. If you are uncertain that you can afford saving more, take a small step. Then mark on your calendar a time each year to increase that amount—if your company does not have a feature that would automatically do that for you. Since many plan participants don't look at their retirement plans for years at a time, many don't even know how much they are saving. Is it 3 percent, 7 percent, 10 percent, 15 percent, or 20 percent?

Do *you* know how much you are saving if you are already in your organization's retirement plan?

CHAPTER
SIX

HOW SHOULD YOU INVEST YOUR MONEY?

Choosing how to invest your money in a retirement plan can seem confusing and daunting. Participants in a 401(k) plan are confronted not only with many options but also with a whole new vocabulary of terms and investment concepts that they might have never even known existed.

On top of that, investors are asked to read a prospectus, which is the document that describes and governs the investment vehicle they may be investing in. This document tells people they could lose money and that nothing is guaranteed. In most cases, since markets go in up-and-down cycles, from time to time some investors will lose money.

People also get concerned, scared, and frustrated because, most of the time, they must make their own investment decisions. As an investor in a 401(k) plan, you are typically responsible for the decisions you make and the outcomes you get. The company you work for and the resources you have available almost always provide education regarding these decisions, but you are the ultimate decision-maker.

However, if we are to get anywhere in life, if we are to grow and learn, we have to take risks. It's the same with money if we are to stay ahead of inflation.

In this chapter, I'll briefly describe the structure of the general or basic groups of investment vehicles and then look at three specific types or groups of investment vehicles that may help the new or average investor. If you are a rocket scientist in this realm and enjoy investing your own money, this chapter might be a little too basic for you, so be forewarned. If you are a novice investor, it will provide a good foundation for you. Let's get going!

First, I will define what a mutual fund is and how there are various other similar types of investment vehicles that a participant gets to choose from when investing in a retirement plan. While most mutual funds are based on a single type of asset, such as stocks or bonds, the options discussed here are funds or investment vehicles that offer more diversification.

Then I'll discuss three types of mutual funds or investment choices that add simplicity to the investment process for individuals who want to set it and forget it—even though you may not really *want* to forget what could be one of your greatest assets over time and in your life. This section will include a discussion of target-date funds, lifestyle funds (risk-based funds), and managed accounts within retirement plans.

Mutual Funds

Most company retirement plans provide an array of mutual funds as options. Mutual funds are investment vehicles that invest in a collection of stocks (securities representing a share of the ownership in companies, which also may be referred to as equities), bonds (the debt of companies or governments), and cash (such as a money-market fund or a guaranteed investment pool). These pools of investments are often referred to as a portfolio.

A "mutual fund" is a specific type of investment vehicle that was created under the Investment Company Act of 1940. Today, many plans have similar types of investment vehicles that may be referred to as "comingled pools" or collective investment trusts. Some plans may also offer other types of investment vehicles.

For our purposes, we can simply refer to all of these as *mutual funds*. If you are interested in the technical legal distinctions among these products, please research them on the web or consult an attorney familiar with investments. If you are interested in *exactly* what you are investing in, please refer to your company's service provider or your plan sponsor to obtain and read all the required documents that must be made available to you as an investor. The government requires that these documents be made available to you and encourages you to read them before investing.

What Are Mutual Funds?

Mutual funds have six basic traits.

1. They are **pools of money** from many different investors put together in one account or portfolio. The investors may be retirement plan participants, individuals, institutions, etc.

2. They are **professionally managed**. Mutual funds are typically managed by a specific individual or a team whose full-time job is to manage these funds. These people are highly educated and trained in this profession, and they

have the technology and tools to hopefully make wise investment decisions.

3. They are **managed to meet a specific investment objective**, such as growth, growth with income, income, or stability of principle. A growth portfolio normally invests in stocks. Growth and income portfolios tend to invest in bonds and in companies that often pay dividends or cash out to investors on a regular basis. Income portfolios usually invest in bonds. Stability-of-principle funds typically invest in short-term debt vehicles. Many funds seeking stability of principle may be called "money-market funds" or be referred to as "guaranteed income." (Please be aware that guaranteed products are usually *not* guaranteed by your company or the US government but by an insurance company that manages this pool of money.) Some funds may be index funds, in that they seek to replicate the performance of a well-known index such as the Standard & Poor's 500 Stock Index. These funds may be managed by a computer; however, they may have a portfolio manager assigned to them so someone can be held accountable for their performance. These types of funds are referred to as "nonactively managed funds."

4. They offer **diversification**. Mutual funds usually hold many securities. This makes them a cost-efficient way for many investors to get market exposure and invest across many securities, which they might not be able to do on their own.

5. They offer **liquidity**. This means you can usually buy or sell them on a daily basis. However, retirement plan investors should be thinking long term and not be trading daily.

6. By design, they are **an affordable way to invest**, in that you do not have to hire a personal investment manager and pay a variety of other fees. This we will address more in a later chapter.

Target-Date Funds, Lifestyle Funds (Risk-Based Funds), and Managed Accounts

To help retirement plan participants, most 401(k) retirement plans may offer one of the following types of investment vehicles:

- **Target-date funds.** A target-date fund is a mutual fund that automatically remixes the stocks, bonds, and cash equivalents in its portfolio so that the portfolio gets more conservative as you get closer to your retirement date (the investor's "time horizon").

- **Lifestyle or risk-based funds.** A lifestyle, or risk-based, fund is a mutual fund that is usually based on a person's tolerance for risk. Investors usually choose a fund with "conservative," "moderate," "growth," or "aggressive growth" in the title. Often providers offer a very simple questionnaire to help participants determine which fund might be best for them. These funds maintain the same risk level over time.

- **Managed accounts.** These are usually designed and tailored to a person's specific situation, which is determined after completing a questionnaire. Then the money within the retirement plan is allocated to a variety of specific funds within the plan. Managed accounts may maintain the same risk level over time or may become more conservative as one approaches retirement. Often, there may be an additional fee associated with managed accounts.

Target-Date Funds (TDF)

Target-date funds are the most popular vehicle within retirement plans today. One major record keeper for retirement plans reported, for example, that 90 percent of their plans at the end of 2015 offered target-date funds.[15]

Target-date funds offer an asset-allocation mix based on the year you expect to retire, so the risk level of the portfolio decreases as you get closer to retirement. The asset-allocation mix refers to how the funds are invested as far as more risk-based assets, stocks, and more conservative assets such as bonds (again, the debt instruments of companies or government). The funds with dates further in the future often have more stocks in them than bonds because investors can usually take more risks with their investments when they are younger.

The target date is the approximate date when investors plan to start withdrawing their money. The principal value of a target date fund is not guaranteed at any time, including at the target date; and the funds' objectives change over time.

This asset-allocation mix changes over time by the company managing the funds. This type of fund is attractive to many investors because the allocation changes without them having to do anything.

---

15   Jean A. Young and John A. Lamancusa, "TDF adoption in 2015," Vanguard Center for Retirement Research, 2016.

Age has been found to be one of the most significant determinants in setting an investment strategy and asset allocation for individuals.

The change in the asset allocation over time is called a "strategic allocation" because it changes as you approach retirement, almost always becoming more conservative. This change is known as the "glidepath."

These funds are not 100 percent risk-free when you retire. Given that most people are expected to live another thirty years after they retire, a good portion of these funds will still be invested in stocks. This means there will be volatility, and the swings of the market will affect the value of your portfolio. Remember, you still need to keep your investments growing at a good rate after you retire so that your buying power is not diminished by inflation. From this perspective, having some risk in your portfolio is good.

Lifestyle Funds (Risk-Based Funds)

Lifestyle funds, which may also be referred to as risk-based funds, are also very popular in 401(k) plans and are based on the level of risk and return that is appropriate for a plan participant's risk tolerance. Lifestyle funds typically maintain a given level of risk over time.

Factors determining which specific fund might be appropriate for an investor at a given time include one's age, his or her tolerance for a decline in their portfolio, how secure they feel about how much they have already saved, and how close they are to retirement.

Usually, plan participants will see a range of funds being featured as conservative, moderate, growth, or aggressive growth funds.

Often a company or a company's service provider might include a short, simple quiz to help employees and plan participants determine their risk tolerance. Here is a sample illustration from Empower Retirement, one of the leading service providers in the 401(k) industry:

DETERMINE YOUR RISK TOLERANCE

To determine the mix of investments that best meets your retirement needs, first identify your risk comfort level. Complete the survey below by circling the number that best describes how strongly you agree or disagree with each of the statements.

1. I am a knowledgeable investor who understands the trade-off between risk and return and am willing to accept a greater degree of risk for potentially higher returns.

DISAGREE 1   4   5   AGREE

3. If one of my investments dropped 20% in value over six months due to a stock market fluctuation, I would hold on to that investment, expecting it to recover its value.

DISAGREE 1   4   5   AGREE

2. I am willing to invest on a long-term basis.

DISAGREE 1   4   5   AGREE

4. I have savings vehicles other than this account that make me feel secure about my financial future.

DISAGREE 1   4   5   AGREE

Now add up the numbers you circled above to get your Risk Tolerance score:

_____

Use your Risk Tolerance score to help determine your preferred investor type, shown here with the corresponding asset allocation example.

ASSET ALLOCATION   ■ Stock Funds   ■ Cash Equivalents   ■ Bond Funds

Conservative (4–8 points):
You are comfortable with investments that have a lower risk with potentially lower returns. The illustration to the right is an example of a conservative mix of assets.

10% / 30% / 60%

Moderate(9–14 points):
You are comfortable with some volatility. This mix is a balance between lower and higher risk investments. The risk and return potential is greater than the conservative mix, but not as great as the aggressive mix. The illustration to the right is an example of a moderate mix of assets.

5% / 35% / 60%

Aggressive(15–20 points):
You are comfortable with higher risk for potentially higher returns. The illustration to the right is an example of an aggressive mix of assets.

5% / 10% / 85%

For illustrative purposes only. Intended to illustrate possible investment portfolio allocations that represent an investment strategy based on risk and return. This is not intended as financial planning or investment advice.

Copyright by Empower Retirement. Used by permission.

In this illustration, you will see the quiz, a way to determine your risk level, and how a portfolio in each category might be allocated based on your risk tolerance.

While Lifestyle Funds are one way to invest, the concern of some industry experts is that investors might not make the one or two changes to their investments needed to become more conservative as they approach retirement. Another concern is that if the market has just suffered a severe correction or is at an all-time high, plan participants might be subconsciously biased by the news in how they answer questions. This then might affect their quiz results—and which Lifestyle Fund they ultimately choose.

I have found that the vast majority of people I have worked with have ended up in the moderate allocation category that appears to have served them well over time.

Managed Accounts

Plan sponsors are increasingly using or implementing managed accounts in their plans, since several leading consulting and investment firms believe they improve employees' retirement savings.

It is typical with a managed account, that a third party—which could be an outside investment manager or your company's financial advisor or consultant—puts together portfolios for the individuals in the retirement plan based on their investment models. The portfolios for individuals will most likely consist of the mutual funds that are already in a company's 401(k) plan.

To determine what model is best, participants usually have to answer a questionnaire that may consist of many more than four questions.

Managed accounts, therefore, are usually more customized to the needs of the individuals to help them pursue their retirement goals and at the same time understand their tolerance for risk.

Some managed account programs also recommend savings rates for individuals if they are saving below the amount they need for retirement. If they do not do this, they may show only the benefit of saving just 1, 2, or 3 percent more over time. These programs usually seek to remind participants throughout their working years as to how much they should be saving—and the benefits of saving more.

In a later chapter I'll address the question: are you saving enough?

The managed account option is attractive because it takes into account a person's current age and the age at which the participant expects to retire. It is not solely based on a person's risk profile. Companies offering these services may utilize proprietary processes and systems to tailor portfolios to the investors in these products.

Depending on the type of managed account program a plan offers, they may be managed to a set risk level, like the lifestyle funds, or they may become more conservative as one approaches retirement, like the target-date funds.

The downside to managed accounts is that there is no uniformity as to how these funds are managed in the industry—not that there really needs to be—and there is usually an added cost to the participants who choose this option.

You Choose

While it is always your choice in how you invest, and your company may offer many mutual funds, they may offer just one or two of the investment options we have discussed.

Whatever is available to you, these options are usually easy to choose from and a handy way to diversify your assets to help you save for retirement.

If you have only the target-date fund as an option, consider the fund with the date closest to the year you intend to retire.

If your plan offers the lifestyle or risk-based funds, complete the short questionnaire that your plan uses to get an idea of which specific fund you should be considering.

If you have a managed account program and decide that is the best option for you, complete the questionnaire and process associated with that option, and begin your journey.

My personal belief is that all of these investment choices are good options; however, you must remember that no one can accurately predict or control the markets over time.

But, as always, whatever you do, *take action now*!

CHAPTER 6 TAKEAWAYS:

After reading this chapter, if you are new to investing, you should look at your retirement plan and determine which of the three types of asset-allocation funds or investment vehicles your plan has.

- target-date funds

- risk-based or lifestyle funds

- managed accounts

Then based on the year you expect to retire—or after taking a quick quiz or questionnaire—determine where your money should go.

It is that easy.

There is no assurance that these investments are suitable for all investors or will yield positive outcomes. Investing in mutual funds involves risk, including possible loss of principal. Upon redemption, the value of fund shares may be worth more or less than their original cost. Value will fluctuate with market conditions and may not achieve its investment objective.

There is no guarantee that a diversified portfolio will enhance overall returns or outperform a non-diversified portfolio. Diversification does not protect against market risk.

THAT FOUR-LETTER
WORD: FEES

Retirement plan fees are important to understand and review. Fees and expenses paid by the plan, out of plan assets—*your* assets—can significantly reduce the growth in your account and its ability to generate retirement income. Fees and expenses have been found to be the second biggest determinant of investment returns (after asset allocation).

Let me tell you about one participant, John, and his encounter with plan fees and how they affected his account.

Not too long ago, John met with the CEO of the small company for which he worked. He had noticed on the last few statements of his company-based retirement plan that he seemed to be *losing* money, even though he was investing in a relatively low-risk money-market fund. He tried to keep his cool, but the business owner could see his anger and frustration. She stopped what she was doing to find out what was going on—which quickly increased her own frustration.

As you read this, you might be wondering the same thing: Why did it seem that John was losing money? Isn't a money-market fund supposed to maintain a dollar's value and earn interest?

Money-market funds seek to maintain a dollar value and earn interest—though, again, the level of interest is almost never guaranteed. John's money-market fund was doing just that—maintaining that dollar value and paying interest to him as an investor in that fund. However, many employees today are invested in money-market funds and *are* losing money, or at least it appears that they, like John, are losing money.

Why is this?

The answer is that 401(k) plans have expenses, bills that the investor or the sponsoring organization need to pay to keep the plan up and running. In John's case, the plan was taking money out of his account quarterly to pay his plan expenses, so it appeared he was losing money in a money-market fund. It was the fees and expenses that were causing John's shortcomings.

(On a side note, as I write this, interest rates are close to zero. Today, just about everyone in money-market funds is earning very little.)

Someone has to pay the record keeper, or in other words, the company that keeps the records of the plan. Someone has to pay an administrator, often an outside organization that keeps the plan documents and completes the plan's annual filing with the United States Department of Labor. Someone also needs to pay the broker or registered investment advisor for helping you and your plan sponsor with the investments and/or the other requirements that need to be adhered to by law for the operation of the plan. There also might be legal fees and/or accounting fees to help maintain the plan. In short, there are costs involved in running a plan.

Many of these expenses can be taken out of the plan and your account specifically to help cover the plan's overall costs. Often a participant might see this money being subtracted from his or her account on a quarterly basis, and that is what was happening to John. For every dollar John was putting into the plan, he was seeing something like ninety-five cents left. So naturally, he was upset.

So is the plan worth it in this example?

Well, oddly, yes—from three perspectives:

1. If John were in the 25 percent tax bracket and took his money in the form of his pay, in this case, he would only receive about seventy-five cents on the dollar. Here he is receiving ninety-five cents, given he is saving on a pretax basis.

2. In his 401(k), John will also be able to grow his money tax-deferred over time until he retires (although he will have to pay taxes when he pulls the money out). So, from this perspective, he would be better off investing in the plan.

3. In this case, too, the company had a match. It matched dollar for dollar, up to 3 percent of pay, for every dollar John put in. So, in this case, if John put in $1, his company would put in $1.

So even with the expenses of the plan, in this example, John would have a little less than $2 in his account, even after the fees are deducted. This is significantly better than the seventy-five cents John would have walked home with if he had taken his money in pay.

Wouldn't you agree?

I include this example here for illustration purposes only so that you may better understand how fees might affect you. The figures I'm using are estimates only.

To cover the plan costs, fees may be taken out of participant accounts as a flat dollar amount quarterly, such as a $25 quarterly fee (this might be much higher or lower depending on the size of your plan and the costs involved in running it).

In short, the 401(k) plan is actually a great investment vehicle for most.workers today. Again, in John's case, he was saving ninety-five cents on the dollar versus taking home seventy-five cents. Remember, too, that with the company match, he was walking away with a little under $2.00.

Yes, I get it; I too never like to lose money or pay for things I do not see. However, I don't want to leave money on the table either.

The Services

Your organization's 401(k) plan needs to pay for a host of services in order to maintain your retirement plan. Often, these services are never seen by you as the participant, but they still need to be rendered and paid for.

Here are a few of them.

A plan sponsor usually has to hire an **administrator** or **third-party administration service** to help with the initial creation of the plan and with many of the ongoing day-to-day aspects of your retirement plan. These services may include such things as: creating the plan documents; amending or restating the plan documents, if needed; assisting with processing all types of distributions from the plan; assisting with IRS or Department of Labor filings; and preparing employer and employee benefit statements, etc.

Your investments within the plan typically have **investment-management fees** associated with them. These fees compensate the investment manager for his or her time and expertise.

A company's 401(k) plan **record keeper** tracks the assets in the plan. The record-keeping company tracks how your money is invested (which mutual funds your money is allocated to); what type of money is invested—your money (either pretax or after tax) and match money put in by the company; and how your investment grows or declines over time, etc. These firms also provide you and your plan with a lot of other services, such as maintaining the call center and web pages to help inform and educate you about your investments, delivering your account statements, and helping your plan sponsor with administration to ensure the plan is compliant with all the laws and regulations governing it.

A **broker, investment advisor, or retirement plan consultant** (for our purposes we will refer to these professionals as financial advisors) may also be engaged to help you and your plan sponsor. These professionals may be hired to help educate you as a participant; educate and assist the plan sponsors regarding their responsibilities; assist with the selection and monitoring of the plan's investments; assist with the search and evaluation of new vendors (such as a new record keeper); ensure the plan is designed to be competitive with other firms within your industry; and provide support to ensure all plan fees are reasonable. Thirty-five percent of plans offer participants investment

> Thirty-five percent of plans offer participants investment advice, and nearly twice that (68.7 percent of companies) retain an independent investment adviser to provide fiduciary responsibility assistance.
>
> Source: 401khelpcenter.com

advice, and nearly twice that (68.7 percent of companies) retain an independent investment adviser to provide fiduciary responsibility assistance.[16]

An **auditor** may also be required to audit plans with over one hundred employees.

Your firm may also need **legal services and advice**, and the fees for these may also be paid for out-of-plan assets. Legal fees might need to be paid for the creation of customized plan documents and amendments or other special services required by your plan sponsor or administrator.

The plan may also pay for **trustee services** because the plan assets must be held in a trust as required by the Employee Retirement Income Security Act of 1974, known as ERISA, which is the legislation overseeing 401(k) plans.

There are a host of **other services** your company may utilize to help it run the plan. These may be services to help select and monitor the plan investments or to help with the day-to-day running of the plan.

How Are Fees Paid and How Might You See Them?

There are several ways fees might be paid:

- Fees can be **paid for by the organization sponsoring the plan directly**. When fees are paid in this manner, it is referred to as a "hard-dollar payment." Many organizations will pay for the plan's administration or third-party administrator fees this way. If your organization is paying for these services, you will not see them.

---

16   "Benchmark Your 401k Plan – 2015: How does your 401k plan compare with other 401k's?" 401k Help Center, http://www.401khelpcenter.com/benchmarking. html#.V2gDR-YrlWo

- Retirement plan sponsors may also **charge plan participants directly** by having the record keeper withdraw a certain dollar amount from the participants' accounts to pay for plan services. Participants in these types of plans may see this fee coming out of their accounts on their quarterly statements as a service fee. This is what was happening to John.

- Plan participants may also be **charged certain fees directly out of their own plan assets** if they utilize plan services to benefit them specifically (such as a loan-processing fee).

- Many of the services may also be **paid out of the mutual fund fees or plan assets**. These other fees go by such esoteric titles as a 12b-1 fee, a subtransfer agent fee, a wrap fee, and/or asset-based fees, and generally, they go to many of the plan's service providers. Because they are paid out of the investments or plan assets (typically, that is, *your* investments, *your* plan assets) themselves, these fees are also known as "soft-dollar fees." To help equalize the way you pay plan expenses, many firms are seeking to levelize fees from these various methods, so everyone pays for them as an equal percentage of their assets. So if all plan fees equal 1.28 percent of plan assets, the amount taken out of your account will most likely be 1.28 percent. Mind you, you may not see this amount taken out of your account directly, given it may be taken out in various ways. If you are really interested in understanding what these (fee levelization, 12b-1 fees, subtransfer agent fees, wrap fees, etc.) are all about, please go to www.401khelpcenter.com for more information.

At the end of the day, all participants will get a fee-disclosure statement on a regular basis that will show the fees they are paying and the potential impact of those fees on the investments to which they apply. While this statement may not spell out specifically how all the fees are being paid—since the plan sponsor may be picking up some of them—it will show you how the fees you are paying may affect you. This is a required document that all participants must receive.

Who Is Responsible for Monitoring the Fees?

The plan sponsor is ultimately responsible for monitoring and tracking all fees and expenses within your retirement plan.

A retirement plan's sponsor must use care, skill, prudence, and diligence that a prudent person would use by acting:

- solely in the interest of you and your beneficiaries;

- for the exclusive purpose of providing benefits to you and your beneficiaries; and

- to pay the reasonable expenses of administering the plan.

In fact, your plan sponsor should be implementing a formal process to determine if the amount of fees being charged to the plan is reasonable and appropriate. This goes for all service providers when fees are paid out of plan assets: the record keeper, the financial advisor, the third-party administrator, etc.

A plan sponsor or person administering the plan should periodically review the fees, compensation, and expenses paid from the portfolio or plan assets to: (1) ensure compliance with all applicable laws, regulations, and service agreements; and (2) ensure that they are reasonable based upon the services provided and the size and complexity of the portfolio or plan.

What constitutes reasonable fees? It depends on what the service provider is doing for your plan, the size of your plan, and the complexity of the plan's investment portfolio, or strategy, or structure. The more the provider does, the larger the plan, the more complex the plan, the higher the fees may be.

A service provider's fee disclosure alone does not by itself give the plan fiduciary adequate information to assess whether a fee is reasonable. A plan might want to benchmark a service provider's fee against other service providers rendering similar services to similar plans. This allows plan fiduciaries to compare oranges to oranges and, thus, make better decisions.

Since senior executives within most firms have a good amount of money in the plan, it also serves them well to keep fees reasonable by monitoring them closely.

Most plan sponsors do their best to monitor and track all fees. If you happen to be a plan sponsor reading this, you just need to remember to *document, document, document* your reasoning and process for selecting and monitoring all service providers in case of an IRS or Department of Labor audit. Your company's plan documentation should summarize all parties being paid from the plan and plan assets, plus it should record and report how much has been paid.

Plan fiduciaries might want to periodically solicit and review bids from at least three service providers to obtain fee and expense data and/or hire an independent consultant to conduct the search and make appropriate recommendations.

What Are Typical Plan Fees?

While this is a good question, it is very hard to answer. There are so many variables, that to state that a plan typically just pays a certain amount in fees is unrealistic.

Remember: plan fees need to be documented as reasonable.

To do that, many plan sponsors will research other service providers and vendors every three to five years to ensure the services they are receiving are still appropriate and that the fees they are paying are reasonable. Often, this is done by conducting a formal and documented search.

On a yearly or even quarterly basis, many plan sponsors will also track and monitor the expenses and performance of the investments within their plan. Annually, between more formal searches, they will also use industry benchmarking services to review fees for their other service providers and their plan's overall costs.

One such service some plan sponsors use on a yearly basis is the *401k Averages Book*, which is a book that has been published since 1995. It claims to be "the oldest, most recognized for nonbiased, comparative 401(k) average cost information." It is used by plan sponsors and financial professionals to determine if plan costs are at, above, or below average.

In the following table, utilizing information from the sixteenth edition of this book, you can see that the spread of plan fees for the various plan sizes—based on assets and the number of participants—can be wide ranging. You will also see that the average cost of a smaller plan is significantly higher than a larger plan. That is because smaller plans must adhere to all the same rules, regulations, and laws as larger plans.

PLAN ASSET SIZE	NUMBER OF PARTICIPANTS	INVESTMENT AND AVERAGE TOTAL BUNDLED COSTS	INVESTMENT AND TOTAL BUNDLED COSTS – HIGHEST	INVESTMENT AND TOTAL BUNDLED COSTS - LOWEST
$500,000	10	1.89 percent	2.60 percent	1.05 percent
$2.5 million	50	1.43 percent	1.87 percent	0.47 percent
$10 million	200	1.14 percent	1.51 percent	0.37 percent

Source: *401k Averages Book*; 16th Edition; 2016 Pension Data Source, Inc.; www.401ksource.com

Here "Investment and Average Total Bundled Costs" is the total of all plan costs. The figures in the table illustrate the costs as a percentage of all plan assets.

After having worked in this industry for many years, those plan sponsors at the highest end of the spectrum might be asleep at the wheel while those on the low end may not be utilizing some of the services that really might benefit their plan.

If you are curious about what your total plan costs might be, ask your plan sponsor. If, for some reason, he or she does not tell you, you should be able to determine how fees impact you by reviewing your participant fee disclosure statement, which your plan sponsor must provide to you on a regular basis.

Potential Benefits of 401(k) Investing—Even with Fees

Some readers might say these fees are extremely high; however, fees are relative. I liken them to three boxes. You see, if life is like three boxes, one box will always be bigger than the next. If you are the middle box, someone will always be bigger than you, smarter than you, and maybe more talented than you in certain areas. If you look around, you will also find someone a little smaller than you, less intelligent than you, and maybe less talented than you. This is just a fact of life. It is the same thing with investment fees and the fees associated with your retirement plan. They are relative.

Several years ago, for example, I worked with a firm that had been sending all its employees' retirement money out to individual retirement accounts at several local brokerage firms. The company was doing this so that it did not have to worry about all the compliance issues and fees associated with running its retirement plan. Unfortunately, it was a pain in the neck to administer the distributions to all the brokers and a costly manual human resource process for the company. Then a new controller for the company came on board. He quickly realized that while the employees had more investment options than they might have in a typical retirement plan, most employees were paying up-front loads or sales charges for all their investments. Some were paying around 5 percent sales fees on top of the annual investment-management fees.

It was my pleasure to help the new controller reconstitute his company's 401(k) plan to help the company's employees. Today, these employees are paying only approximately 1.25 percent yearly in total fees for the benefit of the company's retirement plan. To help keep the plan fees low, the company is also picking up the plan's administrative fees.

Another benefit of a 401(k) plan is that it offers a wide selection of funds to help a company's employees stay ahead of inflation in retirement planning. In addition, it allows people like John, who we discussed earlier in this chapter, to take advantage of the company's match and the benefit of pretax savings.

Remember, too, your plan sponsor usually has his or her own interest at stake when it comes to fees. The people involved tend to watch these very closely because the executives at a company are typically participants, too.

That said, the small-business owner has some challenges, given the number of services needed to provide a well-run 401(k) plan. Many companies will pay the fees directly. This is one benefit many employers never mention to their employees, because it is often too hard to explain all the fees and services associated with a plan.

Also remember that the benefits of a 401(k) plan include allowing you to save money effectively and effortlessly through payroll deductions. A 401(k) offers a variety of investment vehicles to help you stay ahead of inflation. And it is overseen by a fiduciary, a person who takes full responsibility for the operation of the plan.

A 401(k) also allows your money to grow and compound tax-free; that same money invested at a brokerage firm or in a bank would likely be in a taxable account, meaning you would probably be paying taxes on your earnings and dividends every year until you retire.

An investment in a money market fund is not insured or guaranteed by the Federal Deposit Insurance Corporation or any other government agency. Although the Fund seeks to preserve the value of your investment at $1.00 per share, it is possible to lose money by investing in the Fund.

CHAPTER 7 TAKEAWAYS:

Now, don't lose sleep over retirement plan fees. Why?

- Your plan sponsor—usually the owner or one or more officers of your company—is acting as plan trustee. The people involved are legally responsible for documenting and reviewing all plan fees as reasonable on a regular basis. This includes all the money that might be taken out of the plan to pay for your plan's record keeper, advisor, consultant, etc.

- The plan and its trustees could also be audited at any time by the IRS or the US Department of Labor for any reason, or just randomly, and be asked for this documentation.

- Your senior executives most likely have the largest share of their money in the plan, so it is also in their best interest to monitor and keep these fees reasonable.

Laws and regulations are designed to make your retirement plan an easy and very affordable way to help you save for retirement. Retirement plans are a true benefit.

ARE YOU ON TRACK?

Are you on track? It's another million- or multimillion-dollar question for people planning for their retirement.

Many people are not. In fact, they are falling far short of having enough money for retirement.

But when you try to determine where you are with your retirement planning—depending on what you read or who you talk to in the investment industry—you will find there can be multiple answers. Some sources want to specify an exact dollar figure that you should have; some want to use a multiplier of your current income and your age to calculate if you are on track; still others tell you how much monthly income you will need to have in retirement. And some won't give you a definite answer at all.

In this chapter, I'll simplify the process by looking at the number of years that your savings might support you in retirement—based on how much you have saved up to this point, how much you are currently saving, your current age, and at what age you might retire.

I'll make this process easy by referring to an online financial calculator. Those of you looking for a good guide should find this chapter helpful in giving you a great start to see if you are on track to have enough money in retirement.

Please note: I cannot tell you definitely if you are saving enough for a comfortable retirement without making several assumptions. In fact, nobody can. (Your money, most likely, will not grow consistently in a straight line, and I'll address that in the next chapter.)

(Also note that the information here is primarily for persons with a relatively long way to go until retirement. I encourage those of you who are closer to retirement or who have significant assets to go to a financial planner and pay for a financial plan. They will not only look at your retirement savings but at your assets overall.)

In order to calculate how much you'll need in retirement, let's make several assumptions.

We need to make assumptions about how much your income (paycheck) will grow each year, how much your money will grow each year before and after retirement, and what the rate of inflation will be.

Let's use what are probably realistic assumptions—what you have saved up to this point and how many years that money could last you in retirement. I have done this with hundreds of people and have found that *most of them can only live for about five years in retirement on the money they have saved.* This is a major shock to most of the people I have met with. That is why other retirement books get people who are close to retirement thinking about working longer, working part time in retirement, and saving a great deal more now.

For your annual income growth, we will assume a 3 percent growth because that is how much it has generally grown in the recent past. Similarly, we will assume your money in the retirement plan will grow consistently at 7 percent before you retire, at 4 percent after you retire, and that inflation will be 3 percent annually throughout your life.[17]

In addition, taking a quick back-of-the-envelope calculation, let's assume that you will live on 3 percent of your retirement savings yearly. For some people though, that figure may not be completely accurate. Based on the amount of retirement savings you currently have, if you took 3 percent of your retirement savings yearly, would you be able to live on that amount?

Since the focus of this book is on people who are still a number of years from retirement, I encourage you to save considerably more now and work longer, given your likelihood of living longer than the many generations before you.

What about the Income Replacement Value I See on My 401(k) Statement?

Thousands of individuals get quarterly statements stating how much income their savings will get them in retirement.

What about that number? To be honest, I personally don't know how relevant that number is nor all the assumptions that are being made to calculate that number. If you check with the company providing those numbers, you may be able to get a better understanding of how they are calculated.

For our purposes in this book, I have a simple, straightforward way to give you a better sense—a realistic sense—of whether you are really saving enough or not. If you want to calculate your own number, I would suggest using an online retirement calculator like

---

17 This is a hypothetical example and is not representative of any specific situation. Your results will vary. The hypothetical rates of return used do not reflect the deduction of fees and charges inherent to investing.

the one at Bankrate.com. This calculator clearly identifies the assumptions it uses to produce the results in graphical and statistical form.

Now you might ask, why focus on how long your money will last in retirement versus how much income you will have in retirement? Because it will give you a more realistic sense of whether you really are saving enough.

Now, let's get to the numbers and the assumptions you will need to calculate how many years your money will last you in retirement. Here, I'll also walk through an example.

You will need to know the following:

How old are you now? In our example, we will assume thirty-five.

What is your salary? Only you can answer this question. Most of you know this number, but those of you who live paycheck to paycheck may have to look at last year's tax return. In this example, the hypothetical yearly salary is $40,000.

How much are you currently saving? Again, most of you should know this number. If not, check with the company that provides you with your quarterly statement. You should be able to call them or you may be able to check your account online. For the example here, I'll use 8 percent.

What will be the rate of inflation? We would all like this number to remain low, around 2 or 3 percent. Over the last one hundred years, however, it has averaged closer to 3 percent. So the examples in this chapter (and most of this book) are based on 3 percent.

What will my investment returns be going forward? Who knows! Most industry experts are now assuming an annual rate of 7 percent before a person retires. I think this is reasonable and more on the mark than the 10 percent assumptions that were being made when I entered the workforce.

When will you retire? Once again, I believe it is very reasonable for a younger person to think about retiring at age seventy, seventy-five, or even later. I just think we now live in a world where retiring at sixty-five is a thing of the past. So in the example here, we'll assume your retirement age to be seventy-five.

What will my rate of return be after I retire? I admit that trying to predict exactly what's going to happen thirty, forty, or fifty years from now may be a bit unrealistic. For the purposes of our example, though, let's assume 4 percent—given that you don't want to take a ton of risk with your money when you retire.

How many years will you live in retirement? Please take a guess. I have reason to believe my life expectancy may be over one hundred. For younger people, I would encourage you to think about one hundred. For this example, I'll use one hundred. So if you retire at seventy-five and live to one hundred, you will need twenty-five years of retirement income.

What percent of my current income will I need to have in retirement? Who knows? For now, let's go with 90 percent; that's 90 percent of your current income. (Since this book is designed for people who will be retiring thirty, forty, or fifty years from now, to make realistic assumptions on what everything will cost may be close to impossible. So it's probably better not to try to create an in-depth retirement budget right now.)

Let's review and list the assumptions:

- current age: 35

- age of retirement: 75

- annual household income: $40,000

- annual retirement savings: 8 percent
- current retirement savings (what you have saved up until this point in time): $25,000
- expected income increases: 3 percent
- income required at retirement: 90 percent
- years of retirement income: 25
- rate of return before retirement: 7 percent
- rate of return during retirement: 4 percent
- expected rate of inflation: 3 percent

Note: This calculator also has a [+] button that will produce a dropdown allowing you to select whether you are married and if you want to include Social Security income in your calculation, in case you feel confident it will still be around. For now, don't check either of these options.

So now, using the Bankrate.com calculator, enter the afore-mentioned numbers in the required fields and press the "calculate" button. Your results show that you will have enough saved to live to eighty-six years of age.

Unfortunately, according to the calculator, you're not going to have enough to live on for the duration of your estimated lifespan. You may also notice that 90 percent of $40,000 in retirement buying power is $114,013. If this seems outrageous, please go back and review the chapter on compound interest and inflation (chapter 3).

RETIREMENT SAVINGS RUNS OUT AT AGE 86

Your plan provides $1,216,094 when you retire. This assumes annual retirement expenses of $114,013 which is 90% of your last year's income of $126,681. This includes $0 per year from Social Security.

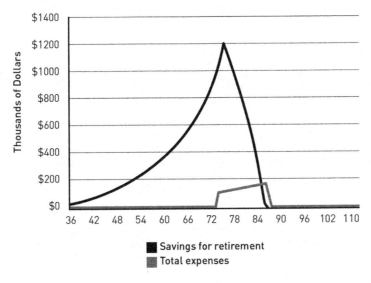

Source: ©KJE Computer Solutions, LLC. Financial Calculators 1998–2015.

Remember, though, this is an estimate; life doesn't always operate perfectly or mathematically.

But assuming that the calculations are correct—or nearly so—what do you need to do?

Well, for starters, it is clear that you are not saving enough. In fact, you will need to increase your savings to 20 percent to have enough money in retirement. Here are the results using the same calculator but entering 20 percent in the "Annual retirement savings" data field.

RETIREMENT SAVINGS AND EXPENDITURES

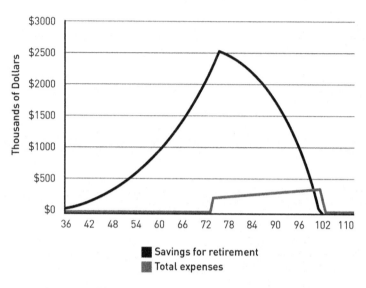

Savings for retirement
Total expenses

Source: ©KJE Computer Solutions, LLC. Financial Calculators 1998–2015.

Perhaps now you can see why beginning early is so important.

If you think my numbers are extreme, you don't agree with them, or perhaps they don't make sense for your life situation, then go ahead and make your own calculations using different assumptions.

Just do it. Start taking control of your financial life. It's up to you.

One Final Action Item

Please take the time to select the "view report" button on this calculator. Then print the report off, date it, save it, and refer to it in a year to see if you are on track.

This will go a long way in helping you pursue your retirement savings goal.

Note: This is only one of many great online retirement calculators. Please use this one and others to help you determine if you are saving enough. Be sure to print off your reports so you can review them on a regular basis to get a better understanding of the assumptions you are making and get a visual of whether you are on track. I suggest you save these estimates and calculations to review them at least annually.

Please also engage a financial professional, if you can, to help you.

CHAPTER 8 TAKEAWAYS:

This is a critical chapter since our minds tend to protect us and tell us "we're all set" when we are not. So you need to take a step back and get the facts.

After reading this chapter you may want to:

1. Reread the chapter and write down all the numbers you will need to use and complete the retirement calculator. If you are unsure about doing this or the amounts you should be using, take a best guess. You may also want to consult the financial professional working with your company or one of your company's service providers.

2. Go online and use a retirement calculator. If this is your first time using this type of tool, don't be surprised if you're only on track to have one or two years of retirement money saved.

3. Determine if you can increase your retirement saving amount. If you can, even by a little, go for it. Contact your company's service provider or your human resources department and see what you need to do.

4. Print the results of your calculations (the report) or save it electronically so you can revisit it in the future. Make sure you date it, so you can track your progress.

5. If you panic or need help, please take a positive step and seek the aid of a financial advisor. You are not alone.

CHAPTER
NINE

SIGN UP, MENTAL REFRAMING, AND UNDERSTANDING YOUR SPECIFIC RETIREMENT PLAN

Now let's talk about how to get involved in your company's retirement plan and how to maintain the best mind-set to continue participating for the long term. To do this, I'll quickly review how to sign up for your retirement plan, if you have not done so already. I'll also discuss how to reframe your thinking during market declines, so that you don't become a lemming making bad investment decisions; and I'll discuss a resource where you can find additional information on your organization's retirement plan.

How to Sign Up

There are two major ways that you can be enrolled in a retirement plan. The first way is that you may have to complete a hard copy or online form (which may include the option to enroll via your smartphone). The second is automatic—your company may enroll you without you having to do anything.

Option 1: You do it.

By now, you may already be enrolled. If not, these three steps, once again, are easy.

1. Contact your company's benefits professional and see what specific steps you may need to take. You may need to fill out a form or sign up online via your computer or smartphone. Whatever you need to do, take this step today.

2. Decide how much you want to invest. Start with what you think you can save and, then, try to save a little more annually or when you can. We will all most likely need every penny we can save now for our retirement years. If you can only save 1 percent, try to do so. When you enroll, ask the person assisting you how often you can change your contribution amount, up or down. You may find you can change it whenever you want or need to. Also note that it may take one or two payroll cycles for you to see a change in your paycheck.

3. Decide how you want to invest your money. To make it easier, see if the options discussed in chapter 6 are available to you: target-date funds, lifestyle or risk-based funds, or managed accounts.

Also ask your benefits professional or the person you are talking with for a beneficiary form so that, in case you die, your money can go directly to the person, people, or organization you choose. Completing this form will save your loved ones a lot of hassle collecting this benefit.

That's it! That's how easy it is for you to sign up on your own.

Option 2: Your company does it for you with auto-enroll, auto-increase, and auto-invest.

Your company may have an automatic enrollment process. This process may include an annual automatic escalation amount for your payroll deferral and may automatically choose an appropriate investment vehicle for you.

Nearly half of plans (47.2 percent) have an automatic-enrollment feature. More than half of plans (51.8 percent) have a default deferral of 3 percent, and more than half (57.9 percent) of automatic-enrollment plans also

> Nearly half of plans (47.2 percent) have an automatic-enrollment feature. More than half of plans (51.8 percent) have a default deferral of 3 percent, and more than half (57.9 percent) of automatic-enrollment plans also automatically increase default deferral rates. Seventy-two percent of plans default to target-date funds.

increase default deferral rates automatically. Seventy-two percent of plans default to target-date funds.[18]

Automatic enrollment, increase, and investment are simple; you have to do very little work.

While some may believe this is a form of intrusion into one's personal decision-making process, this method is meant to help you—given the pervasive lack of understanding concerning what we all need to do to have enough money in retirement.

In an automatic option, your company may enroll you on a certain date, at a certain savings amount, and in a certain type of investment. Once done, you will see your money automatically being taken out of your paycheck. Then, with auto-increase, the company may take an additional 1 percent of your pay every year and put it into your retirement account. Remember, this is still *your* money; it's being put into *your* retirement account.

Your organization must give you advance notice that it will be automatically enrolling you into the plan on a certain date, at a certain amount, and in a certain investment vehicle. In addition, the company must also give you the opportunity to opt out.

One company I visited several years ago had the best plan I have ever seen. While many plans utilizing the auto-enrollment and auto-increase methods start their employees off at a 3 percent savings rate and then increase it 1 percent annually, this company started deducting 8 percent of its employees' pay into the company's retirement plan after each new employee had been with the company for six months. It then increased this amount 1 percent each year after that until the amount being deducted from the employees' paycheck hit 15 percent.

---

18   Benchmark Your 401k Plan – 2015, 401khelpcenter,
http://www.401khelpcenter.com/benchmarking.html#.VlHgTb8Qjm5.

When the chief financial officer of the company told me this, I almost fell out of my chair. At that point, I had to ask him several questions.

The first question was: Why so much? He explained that many of the company's employees had never graduated from high school or at best only had a high school degree, and the company's leaders wanted the employees to work for the company for their entire working career. The CFO stated that the company saw its employees as family and it wanted to help them as much as it could now, to potentially ensure they would have enough money for retirement. He explained that the company knew the likelihood of its employees having enough in retirement without this type of plan was very slim, so the company wanted to set them up for success.

I then asked if they had much pushback from their employees. He said no. The plan was sold as a benefit in the hiring process and the older employees raved about it to the younger and newer employees. By doing this and presenting it as a great benefit, a great attitude about saving for retirement permeated the company.

This completely shocked me. The company was doing the right thing for the right reasons. It understood that many employees don't really comprehend all the complexities of investing, compound interest, and the time value of money, so it took the steps it believed were necessary to help its employees.

This company is probably one in a million that is doing something like this. At this point, if your company is even starting you out at 3 percent, be grateful. It is trying to be proactive in helping you save for retirement.

If your company is not doing something similarly as aggressive, be grateful your company has a retirement plan at all. Then think about setting yourself up for success by contemplating, planning, and scheduling your own retirement plan for success.

Think about increasing your savings amount today to get you on a better track, then increasing it by 1 percent a year until you hit 15 or 20 percent—if you feel that amount is right for you. Hopefully, your savings rate is or will be between 10 and 20 percent in the future. If you do this, schedule your increase in your calendar once a year. Many people who are on this success track schedule this increase to occur around the time of their annual salary increase, so it potentially does not decrease their take-home pay.

> Decide and act: What is best for you? What can you do? What do you want to do? Take action! Make it happen!

Decide and act. What is best for you? What can you do? What do you want to do? Take action! Make it happen!

Mental Reframing

As human beings, we are often driven by our primitive brain. This is the part that will fight, freeze, or run when we are frightened.

When markets decline and our investments fall in value, our primitive mind often gets scared, confused, and worried about our financial future. This is normal. This fear is then exacerbated by the things we read in the news. Our mirror neurons subconsciously also pick up the fear in the photos we see of scared, frustrated, and worried investment professionals or traders. Our primitive mind may also go into overdrive when we look at the activity in our own accounts.

It is our primitive mind that also goes into overdrive when the market roars upward during bull markets, as we excitedly compound that growth hypothetically and mentally into the future. During periods like these, which may last for years—as they almost always do during both stock and housing booms—our minds tend to negate downside risk and take on more risk than we really should. During roaring bull markets, typically all we see are huge gains.

Therefore, many investors tend to do the opposite of what they should do and buy high and sell low. This devastates our investments and can ruin our financial future. In fact, most investors end up with returns far short of what a diversified portfolio might return.

J.P. Morgan, a Wall Street investment firm, with the aid of Morningstar Direct, DALBAR, Inc., and J.P. Morgan Asset Management, regularly publish charts illustrating how the average investor, over the last twenty years, has obtained mediocre returns versus the overall market returns in a hypothetical balanced investment account. In fact, from 1996 to 2015, the average investor has only earned 2.1 percent annually on his or her investment. This versus 8.2 percent annually for the overall market (as measured by the Standard & Poor's 500 Stock Index [S&P 500]) and 6.7 percent annually in a diversified account (holding 60 percent in stocks, as measured by the S&P 500 and 40 percent in high-quality US fixed-income securities, as measured by the Barclays US Aggregate Index).

20-YEAR ANNUALIZED RETURNS BY ASSET CLASS (1996-2015)

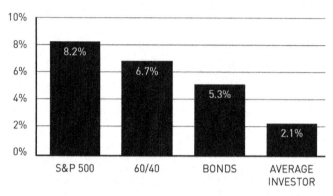

Source: J.P. Morgan Asset Management, Dalbar inc. Indexes used are as follows: 60/40: A balanced portfolio with 60% invested in S&P 500 Index and 40% invested high quality U.S. fixed income, represented by the Barclays U.S. Aggregate Index. The portfolio is rebalanced annually. Average asset allocation investor return is based on an analysis by Dalbar Inc., which utilizes the net of aggregate mutual fund sales, redemptions and exchanges each month as a measure of investor behavior. Returns are annualized (and total return where applicable) and represent the 20-year Guide to the Markets – U.S. Data are as of May 31, 2016. DALBAR'S 2015 Quantitative Analysis of Investor Behavior (QAIB) study examines real investor returns from equity, fixed income and money market mutual funds from January 1984 through December 2014. The study was originally conducted by DALBAR, Inc. in 1994 and was the first to investigate how mutual fund investors' behavior affects the returns they actually earn. Past performance is no guarantee of future results. Indexes cannot be invested into directly.

Think about that: 2.1 percent annually versus 8.2 percent and 6.7 percent annually.

To negate this, you need to think differently about every market correction or advancement. To do this, utilize one of the mental techniques mentioned in chapter 2. During extreme times, think:

THIS TOO WILL PASS.

Given that many investors get scared and sell when the market is down, you must first remind yourself that, over time, the market has done well. In fact, J.P. Morgan regularly points out that the market has been up twenty-seven of the past thirty-six years, as measured by the S&P 500. Second, remind yourself that markets go down regularly during "up" years. In fact, this index has had an average intra-year drop of 14.2 percent (over the last thirty six years: 1980 through 2015).

It's normal for the market to correct (go down) on a very regular basis. In fact, drops during any calendar year historically may be significant or small. In 2008, the S&P 500 fell approximately 38 percent. In 1994, it fell 2 percent. For more aggressive investors, these declines may be even greater.

So when the market declines, you must reframe your mind and not get scared. Instead tell yourself that, historically, this is normal and most likely:

THIS TOO WILL PASS.

Some investors who get good at this mind-reframing technique may even see these downturns as a good time to invest additional money, if they have it, so they end up investing more money during market declines than when the market is advancing.

Please take a minute and look and study the following table. It shows what the S&P 500 Stock Index returned for the last fifteen years and what the largest intra-year decline was for the market. To help reframe your thinking, you may want to pull this out whenever you get fearful of a market decline. You may also want to avoid or filter out the negative news and listen only to those commentators that tell you that market declines are normal. Again, declines will happen, and they may affect us emotionally, psychologically, and potentially even physically, if we do not put them in the right perspective.

S&P 500 INTRA-YEAR DECLINES
VS. CALENDAR YEAR RETURNS

Despite average intra-year drops of 14.2%, annual returns were positive in 27 of the last 35 years*

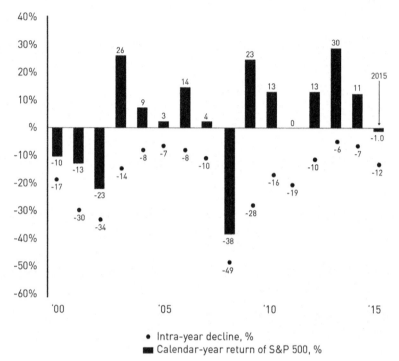

• Intra-year decline, %
■ Calendar-year return of S&P 500, %

Source: FactSet, Standard & Poor's, J.P. Morgan Asset Management.
Returns are based on price index only and do not include dividends. Intra-year drops refer to the largest market drops from a peak to a trough during the year. For illustrative purposes only. *Returns shown are calendar year returns from 2000 to 2015.
Guide to the Markets – U.S. Data are as of December 31, 2015.

So let's remember, for our retirement savings, that investors will see a great deal of market movement. Some of those movements will be dramatic, and for those who sell low, those movements may be devastating.

Understanding Your Specific Retirement Plan

This book has gone light on a lot of the more technical aspects of a 401(k) plan. This was done intentionally, given that my attempt was to cover the basics of investing, which includes the time value of money, inflation, compound returns, and how to sign up. Which means that this book is only one chunk of information you may need to help you persue your retirement goals.

For more technical information about your specific retirement plan, you may want to pick up a copy of your organization's **Summary Plan Description (SPD)**, which your benefits person should make available to you as a participant and distribute to you periodically.

This document will highlight such things as:

- when you are eligible to participate in the plan;

- if your company has an employee match, how much it is, and what the vesting schedule is (when the match money becomes your money);

- your rights under the Employee Retirement Income Security Act (ERISA);

- how you might withdraw your funds (at retirement or rolling the funds over to another account if you leave the company);

- contact information of your plan's sponsor so you can resolve any issues; this may be someone in your company's human resources or benefits department; and

- how to apply for and receive hardship withdrawals (if applicable).

This document is usually less than twenty pages long—though some might be quite lengthy. You may want to keep a hard copy of this document in your files, or a digital copy on your computer or in the cloud for your quick reference.

If you have questions, or find the SPD difficult to decipher, reach out to your plan administrator or call one of your plan's service providers for help.

Throughout the year, you will also receive many regular notices regarding your retirement plan. Please take the time to review them because they may have important information.

CHAPTER 9 TAKEAWAYS:

Remember: The steps to getting involved in your organization's retirement plan are easy:

1. Decide if you want to participate. If yes, then contact your organization's benefits professional and see what you need to do to enroll and then do it.

2. Decide how much you want to invest.

3. Decide how to invest your money.

These three steps are the easy part. The hard parts come when you start accumulating money and other things tempt you to put your money elsewhere. It can also be difficult when the market corrects and you see your savings begin to dwindle. When these things occur, try to reframe your thinking:

- Think about your larger retirement goals and the lifestyle you want in retirement.

- Review the compound-interest table in chapter 3.

- Review the "S&P 500 Intra-year Declines Vs. Calendar Year Returns" chart in this chapter that shows how almost every year has a correction, some bigger than others, but they are normal. Review the chart to see how much the market was down inter-year.

- Also review the "20-year Annualized Returns by Asset Class" chart to see the returns for the market over the last twenty years. Look at how the average investor has done far worse than the market by being fooled by his or her own ego or by their primitive brain taking what he or she believes is corrective action. Remember that taking corrective action can sometimes end up being hurtful compared to staying calm and remaining invested through market cycles.

Also remember to review the plan information you receive on a regular basis:

- Summary Plan Description. This is your owner's manual to your retirement plan.

- Your Personal Annual Statement. This reviews your assets in the plan.

- Your plan's Summary Annual Report. This basically tells you that your plan is a qualified plan. It also tells you the size of your plan and who is administering your plan.

CHAPTER
TEN

YOUR NEXT STEPS

I hope you've found this book to be a clear and a useful tool for helping you understand 401(k) plans. The 401(k) is a simple, easy way to put money aside for retirement, and it's very likely that we will all need this money when we're no longer earning a salary.

In this book, we've talked about some very important concepts, including:

- A 401(k) is typically a company-sponsored retirement plan that allows participants to contribute money through payroll deduction.

- 401(k) funds are invested in a variety of investments, and their objective is to grow over time until the participant pulls the money out at retirement.

- The money can be contributed on a pretax or after-tax basis.

- Employers may match contributions.

- Participants can start small and grow their contribution over time.

- Some plans allow for loans or hardship withdrawals.

- The money contributed belongs to the participant and can be rolled over to another type of account if the participant leaves the company.

- A plan participant leaving an employer typically has four options (and may engage in a combination of these options), each choice offering advantages and disadvantages.

- Plan participants leaving a plan may leave the money in his/her former employer's plan, if permitted; roll over the assets to his/her new employer's plan, if one is available and rollovers are permitted; roll over to an IRA; or cash out the account value.

- Visualizing can help you pursue your retirement goals.

- Compounding is a "magic" way to increase your retirement savings.

- Inflation is the stealth killer of our buying power and wealth.

- To determine your number—the end dollar amount you want saved for retirement—start with the end in mind.

- When calculating your number, the rule of thumb for withdrawals in retirement is 3 percent.

- The minimum amount you should be saving over time is 15 percent.

- Most 401(k) plans invest in mutual funds or similar investment vehicles.

- Most 401(k) retirement plans typically offer one of the three types of asset-allocation investment vehicles: target-date funds, lifestyle or risk-based funds, and managed accounts.

- Fees are a necessary evil in 401(k) plans; they pay for the administration and services being provided to the plan.

- Online calculators are useful tools for helping you determine how much to save.

- There are two ways to enroll and manage your plan: you do it, or your company automatically does it for you.

Now it's time for you to take action. Once you've obtained your enrollment form from your human resources or benefits department, or logged onto the online enrollment system, enrolling in your company's 401(k) plan is as easy as 1, 2, 3.

Step 1: Decide whether you want to participate.

Step 2: Decide how much you want to save or what percentage of your salary you want to contribute.

Step 3: Decide how you want to invest.

CHAPTER 10 TAKEAWAYS:

TAKE ACTION!

ENJOY THE JOURNEY!

ABOUT THE AUTHOR

Bob Everett, Chartered Retirement Planning Counselor® (CRPC®), Professional Plan Consultant™ (PPC™), and Accredited Investment Fiduciary® (AIF®), specializes in wealth management, retirement planning, and retirement plan consulting. His role is to simplify complex financial matters to help clients make well-informed decisions toward greater financial independence, and he works to provide clients with suitable investment strategies and programs to pursue their goals.

During his twenty-five-plus years in the financial-services industry, Bob's clients and associates have included all levels in the investment process, from individuals and retirement plan participants to plan sponsors and portfolio managers at some of the leading investment firms. Because of his experience with investment managers at such firms as Fidelity and John Hancock, he understands the dynamics of portfolio construction. In his ongoing work with plan sponsors, plan participants, and individuals, Bob ensures that clients understand the fundamental issues of the investment decisions before them, including the decisions they need to make to invest wisely and the strategies and investment vehicles appropriate for those needs.

Bob graduated from the College of Wooster (Ohio) with a bachelor's degree in business economics, and he holds securities registrations Series 7, 6, 26, 63, and 66 with LPL Financial. He offers securities through LPL Financial, Member FINRA/SIPC.

Bob enjoys travel, reading, and running. He has lived overseas, run four marathons, and carried the Olympic Torch. He lives in Cambridge, Massachusetts.